Big-Needle Knit
AFGHANS™

Edited by Jeanne Stauffer
Exclusively using Brown Sheep yarns

HOUSE of
WHITE
BIRCHES

PUBLISHERS
SINCE 1947

Big-Needle Knit Afghans™

Editor: Jeanne Stauffer
Associate Editor: Dianne Schmidt
Technical Editor: E. J. Slayton, Diane Zangl
Copy Editors: Michelle Beck, Läna Schurb

Photography: Tammy Christian,
Kelly Heydinger, Christena Green
Photography Stylist: Tammy Nussbaum

Publishing Services Manager: Brenda Gallmeyer
Graphic Arts Supervisor: Ronda Bechinski
Art Director: Brad Snow
Book Design: Jessi Butler
Graphic Artist/Cover Design: Erin Augsburger
Production Assistant: Marj Morgan
Traffic Coordinator: Sandra Beres
Technical Artist: Chad Summers

Chief Executive Officer: John Robinson
Publishing Director: David McKee
Book Marketing Director: Craig Scott
Editorial Director: Vivian Rothe
Publishing Services Director: Brenda R. Wendling

Printed in the United States of America
First Printing: 2004
Library of Congress Number: 2003100520
ISBN: 1-59217-019-6

1 2 3 4 5 6 7 8 9

A Note From **the Editor**

WELCOME!

You'll love knitting afghans on big needles. It's quick, it's easy and it's fun. Each afghan in this book is knit on needles size 10½ and up.

Some designs use bulky yarns and others use multiple strands of worsted or sport-weight yarn. All the yarn used for the afghans in this book is from Brown Sheep Co. They have wonderful cotton and wool yarns in a wide array of colors. Their yarn makes knitting such a pleasure.

Knowing that many knitters like to knit baby blankets for precious little ones, we've included an entire section of baby afghans. You'll also find lots of cozy, comfy throws and many afghans with texture and 3-D flowers. For those who love cables, we've also included gorgeous afghans with wonderful cables. You'll love making cables with big needles because they knit up so quickly.

So, welcome to *Big-Needle Knit Afghans*. Come in and enjoy the fun activity of deciding which afghan to knit first. You'll be surprised at the short amount of time it takes to knit an afghan on large, oversized needles. It won't be long before you're deciding on the second afghan to knit, then the third, the fourth and so on. You'll enjoy every stitch!

Warm regards,

Jeanne Stauffer

CONTENTS

SMALL WONDERS

COZY COMFORTS

FLOWER GARDEN

CLASSY CABLES

APPENDIX

SMALL **WONDERS**

Lollipops

Design by Kennita Tully

Bright-colored 'lollipops,' formed by short rows, line up on a cheery kid's blanket.

Skill Level
Intermediate***

Size
Approximately 30 x 44 inches

Materials
- Brown Sheep Lamb's Pride Bulky, 85 percent wool/15 percent mohair bulky weight yarn (125 yds/4 oz per skein): 3 skeins crème #M10 (MC), 1 skein each supreme purple #M100 (A), limeade #M120 (B), RPM pink #M105 (C), orange you glad #M110 (D), and lemon drop #M155 (E)
- Size 11 (8mm) 29-inch circular needle or size needed to obtain gauge
- Tapestry needle

Gauge
9 sts and 15 rows = 4 inches/10cm in Lollipop pat
To save time, take time to check gauge.

Pattern Stitch
Lollipops
Rows 1, 3, 5, 7, 9, 11, 13 (WS): With MC, purl.
Rows 2, 4, 6, 8, 10, 12: Knit.
Row 14: With CC k11, * turn, sl 1 wyif, k3, turn, p4, k12, rep from * across, end last rep k1 instead of k12.
Row 15: With CC k5, * turn, p4, turn, k3, sl 1 wyif, k12, rep from * across, end last rep k7 instead of k12.
Row 16: With MC k8, * sl 2 wyib, k10, rep from *, end last rep k2 instead of k10.

Rows 17–29: Rep Rows 1–13.
Row 30: With CC k5, * turn, sl 1 wyif, k3, turn, p4, k12, rep from * across, end last rep k7 instead of k12.
Row 31: K11, * turn, p4, turn, k3, sl 1 wyif, k12, rep from * across, end last rep k1 instead of k12.
Row 32: With MC k2, * sl 2 wyib, k10, rep from *, end last rep k8 instead of k10.
Rep Rows 1–32 for pat, following color sequence for lollipop rows.

Pattern Note
Sl all sts purlwise.
Color sequence for lollipop rows (Rows 14, 15, 30 and 31) is 2 rows each of A, B, C, D, E, D, C, B, A.

Blanket
With MC, cast on 60 sts.
[Work Rows 1–32 of Lollipop pat] 4 times, rep Rows 1–29.
Bind off.

Border
With RS facing and E, pick up and k 60 sts along cast-on edge.
Knit 1 row.
Knit 2 rows each D, C, B and A.
Bind off.
Rep border along bound-off edge.
Rep border along side edges, picking up 109 sts instead of 60. ◆

Sweet Scallops

Design by Sue Childress

A simplified version of the Old Shale pattern is used to create a delicate baby afghan.

Skill Level
Easy**

Size
Approximately 35 x 47 inches

Materials
- Brown Sheep Lamb's Pride Superwash Bulky, 100 percent washable wool bulky weight yarn (110 yds/100g per skein): 9 skeins mint cream #SW120
- Size 15 (10mm) 29-inch circular needles or size needed to obtain gauge

Gauge
8 sts and 12 rows = 4 inches/10cm in pat st
To save time, take time to check gauge.

Pattern Notes
Two strands of yarn are held tog throughout afghan.
Circular needles are used to accommodate sts. Do not join; work in rows.
St count varies from row to row.

Afghan
Cast on 70 sts.

Bottom Border
Row 1 (WS): Knit.

Row 2: K2, [yo, k2tog] to last 2 sts, k2.
Row 3: Purl.
Rows 4 and 5: Rep Rows 2 and 3.
Beg pat
Row 1 (RS): K2, [yo, k2tog] twice, k3, *ssk, k9, k2tog, rep from * to last 9 sts, k3, [k2tog, yo] twice, k2. (62 sts)
Rows 2 and 4: Purl.
Row 3: K2, [yo, k2tog] twice, k3, *ssk, k7, k2tog, rep from * to last 9 sts, k3, [k2tog, yo] twice, k2. (54 sts)
Row 5: K2, [yo, k2tog] twice, k3, *ssk, yo, [k1, yo] 5 times, k2tog, rep from * to last 9 sts, k3, [k2tog, yo] twice, k2. (70 sts)
Row 6: Knit.
[Rep Rows 1–6] 20 times.

Top Border
Row 1: K2, [yo, k2tog] twice, k to last 6 sts, [k2tog, yo] twice, k2.
Row 2: Purl.
Rows 3 and 4: Repeat Rows 1 and 2.
Rows 5 and 7: K2, [yo, k2tog] to last 2 sts, k2.
Row 6: Purl.
Bind off knitwise on WS.
Wet block. ◆

Strawberry **Parfait**

Design by Sue Childress

Pastel pink and creamy white combine in a delicious baby blanket.

Skill Level
Easy**

Size
Approximately 36 x 40 inches

Materials
- Brown Sheep Cotton Fleece, 80 percent cotton/20 percent Merino wool light worsted weight yarn (215 yds/100g per skein): 4 skeins pink diamond #CW222 (MC), 2 skeins cotton ball #CW100 (CC)
- Size 19 (15mm) needles or size needed to obtain gauge

Gauge
6 sts and 4 rows = 4 inches/10cm in Fern Lace pat
To save time, take time to check gauge.

Pattern Stitches
A. Checked Border
Rows 1 (WS), 3 and 6: K2, *p2, k2, rep from * across.
Rows 2, 4, 5 and 7: P2, *k2, p2, rep from * across.
Row 8: K2, [p2, k2] to last 8 sts, p2tog, k2, p2, k2.
Rep Rows 1–8 for pat.
B. Fern Lace
Rows 1 and 3 (WS): Purl.
Row 2: K3, *yo, k2, ssk, k2tog, k2, yo, k1, rep from

* to last st, k1.
Row 4: K2, *yo, k2, ssk, k2tog, k2, yo, k1, rep from * to last 2 sts, k2.
Rep Rows 1–4 for pat.

Pattern Notes
Four strands of yarn are held tog throughout afghan.
Borders are worked in CC, center area is MC.
To avoid holes when changing colors, always bring new color up over old. When working side borders, do not dec on Row 8.

Afghan
With CC, cast on 62 sts.
Work 8 rows of Checked Border pat.
Set up pat (WS): With CC k2, p2, k2, with MC work Row 1 of Fern Lace pat, with CC k2, p2, k2.
Keeping 6 sts at each end in Checked Border pat and center in Fern Lace, work even for 14 reps, inc 1 MC st on last row. (56 rows)

Top Border
Cut MC.
Next Row: K2, p2, k2, p to last 6 sts, k2, p2, k2.
Work Rows 2–7 of Border pat.
Row 8: K2, *p2, k2, rep from * across.
Bind off. ◆

Confetti

Design by Frances Hughes

Pastel colors combined with cotton yarn create a blanket that is both soft to the touch and easy on the eyes.

Skill Level
Easy**

Size
Approximately 42 x 45 inches

Materials
- Brown Sheep Cotton Fleece, 80 percent cotton/20 percent Merino wool light worsted weight yarn (215 yds/100g per skein): 3 skeins each: pink diamond #CW222, banana #CW620 and spryte #CW640
- Size 15 (10mm) 24-inch circular needle

Gauge
8 sts and 10 rows = 4 inches/10cm in pat
To save time, take time to check gauge.

Special Abbreviations
C2L (cross 2 left): Pass RH needle behind first st, k 2nd st, then k first st, sl both sts off needle.
C2R (cross 2 right): Pass RH needle in front of first st, p 2nd st, p first st, sl both sts off needle.

Pattern Stitch
Confetti Pattern
Row 1: *K1, p1, rep from * across.
Row 2: *P1, k1, rep from * across.

Rows 3–8: Rep Rows 1–2.
Rows 9, 11 and 13: [K1, p1] 3 times, *[k4, p2, C2L, p2] twice, [k1, p1] 3 times, rep from * to end of row.
Rows 10, 12 and 14: [P1, k1] 3 times, [k2, C2R, k2, p4] twice, [p1, k1] 3 times, rep from * to end of row.
Rows 15, 17 and 19: [K1, p1] 3 times, *[P2, C2L, p2, k4] twice, [k1, p1] 3 times, rep from * to end of row.
Rows 16, 18 and 20: [P1, k1] 3 times, *[p4, k2, C2R, k2] twice, [p1, k1] 3 times, rep from * to end of row.
Rows 21–26: Rep Rows 9–14.
Rep Rows 1–26 for pat.

Afghan
With 1 strand of each color held tog, cast on 84 sts.
[Work Rows 1–26 of Confetti pat] 4 times, rep Rows 1–8.
Bind off loosely. ◆

Morning **Sunlight**

Design by Janet Rehfeldt

Cables and long slip stitches resemble rays of
sunshine on this cheery crib blanket.

Skill Level
Easy**

Size
Approximately 34 x 46 inches

Materials
• Brown Sheep Lamb's Pride Superwash
  Worsted, 100 percent washable wool worsted
  weight yarn (200 yds/100g per skein): 10 skeins
  corn silk #SW13
• Size 17 (13mm) 29-inch circular needle
• Cable needle

Gauge
9½ sts and 10 rows = 4 inches/10cm in pat st
To save time, take time to check gauge.

Special Abbreviation
C3F (cable 3 front): Sl 1 st to cn and hold in
front, k2, k1 from cn.

Pattern Note
Afghan is worked with 3 strands of yarn held tog
throughout.
Circular needle is used to accommodate large number of sts. Do not join, work in rows.

Afghan
With 3 strands held tog, cast on 81 sts.
Knit 4 rows.

Beg pat
Row 1 (RS): K3, p2, sl
1 wyib, p2, k1, *p2, k3,
p2, k1, p2, sl 1 wyib, p2,
k1, rep from * to last 2
sts, k2.
Row 2: K2, p1, k2, sl 1
wyif, k2, p1, *k2, p3, k2,
p1, k2, sl 1 wyif, k2, k1,
rep from * to last 2 sts, k2.
Row 3: K3, p2, k1, p2, k1, *p2, k3, [p2, k1] 3
times, rep from * to last 2 sts, k2.
Row 4: Rep Row 2.
Row 5: K3, p2, sl 1 wyib, p2, k1, *p2, C3F, p2, k1,
p2, sl 1 wyib, p2, k1, rep from * to last 2 sts, k2.
Row 6: [K2, p1] 3 times, *k2, p3, [k2, p1] 3 times,
rep from * to last 2 sts, k2.
Row 7: K3, p2, sl 1 wyib, p2, k1, *p2, k3, p2, k1,
p2, sl 1 wyib, p2, k1, rep from * to last 2 sts, k2.
Row 8: Rep Row 2.
Row 9: K3, p2, k1, p2, k1, *p2, k3, [p2, k1] 3
times, rep from * to last 2 sts, k2.
Row 10: Rep Row 2.
Rep Rows 5–10 until afghan measures approximately
48 inches, ending with Row 8.
Knit 3 rows.
Bind off knitwise on WS. ◆

Little Gems

Design by Janet Rehfeldt

Slip stitches and bright colors make this a blanket that looks as good on the reverse side.

Skill Level
Easy**

Size
Approximately 38 x 50 inches

Materials
• Brown Sheep Lamb's Pride Superwash Bulky, 100 percent washable wool bulky weight yarn (110 yds/100g per skein): 9 skeins white frost #SW11 (MC), 2 skeins each serendipity turquoise #SW36 (A) and saffron #SW14 (C), 1 skein sweeten pink #SW35 (B)
• Size 11 (8mm) 36-inch circular needle

Gauge
14 sts and 23 rows = 4 inches/10cm in pat
To save time, take time to check gauge.

Pattern Stitch
Row 1 (RS): With A k1, *sl 1 wyib, k1, rep from * across.
Row 2: K1, *sl 1 wyif, k1, rep from * across.
Row 3: With MC, knit.
Row 4: Purl.
Row 5: With B k2, *sl 1 wyib, k1, rep from * across, end last rep k2.
Row 6: K2, *sl 1 wyif, k1, rep from * across, end last rep k2.
Rows 7–10: With MC, knit.
Row 11: Rep Row 5.
Row 12: Rep Row 6.
Row 13: With MC, knit.
Row 14: Purl.
Row 15: Rep Row 1.

Row 16: Rep Row 2.
Rows 17–20: With MC, knit.
Row 21: Rep Row 1.
Row 22: Rep Row 2.
Row 23: With MC, knit.
Row 24: Purl.
Row 25: With C, rep Row 5.
Row 26: With C, rep Row 6.
Rows 27–30: With MC, knit.
Row 31: With C, rep Row 5.
Row 32: With C, rep Row 6.
Row 33: With MC, knit.
Row 34: Purl.
Row 35: With A, rep Row 1.
Row 36: With A, rep Row 2.
Rows 37–40: With MC, knit.
Rep Rows 1–40 for pat.

Pattern Notes
Sl all stitches purlwise.
Do not carry CC colors up side edge after color rep is finished. Cut yarn, leaving a 6-inch tail for weaving.

Afghan
With MC, cast on 117 sts.
Knit 1 row.
Work even in pat until afghan measures approximately 46 inches, ending with Row 18 or 38. Bind off.

Border
With MC and RS facing, pick up and k 117 sts along bound-off edge.
Row 1 (WS): Knit.

Continued on page 46

Heart of Mine

Design by Kathy Sasser

Here is a perfect afghan for that special little person who has captured your heart!

Skill Level
Intermediate***

Size
Approximately 32 x 40 inches

Materials
- Brown Sheep Cotton Fleece, 80 percent cotton/20 percent Merino wool light worsted weight yarn (215 yds/100g per skein): 9 skeins coral sunset #CW225
- Size 13 (9mm) 32-inch circular needle or size needed to obtain gauge
- Cable needle

Gauge
9 sts and 17 rows = 4 inches/10cm in Irish Moss pat
To save time, take time to check gauge.

Pattern Stitches
A. Irish Moss
(multiple of 2)
Row 1 (WS) and 2: *K1, p1, rep from * across.
Rows 3 and 4: *P1, k1, rep from * across.
Rep Rows 1–4 for pat.

B. Front Cable
(worked over 8 sts)
Rows 1 and 3 (WS): K1, p6, k1.
Row 2: P1, k6, p1.
Row 4: P1, sl 3 sts to cn and hold in front, k3, k3 from cn.
Rep Rows 1–4 for pat.

C. Back Cable
(worked over 8 sts)
Rows 1 and 3 (WS): K1, p6, k1.
Row 2: P1, k6, p1.
Row 4: P1, sl 3 sts to cn and hold in back, k3, k3 from cn.
Rep Rows 1–4 for pat.

Pattern Notes
Circular needle is used to accommodate sts.
Work in rows, do not join.
Three strands of yarn are held tog throughout afghan.
Work Rows 1–19 of Cabled Heart chart once, [rep Rows 4–19] 7 times.

Continued on page 46

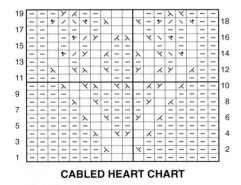

CABLED HEART CHART

STITCH KEY	
☐	K on RS, p on WS
–	P on RS, k on WS
	Sl 1 to cn and hold in front, k1, k1 from cn
	Sl 1 to cn and hold in back, k1, k1 from cn
	Sl 1 to cn and hold in front, p1, k1 from cn
	Sl 1 to cn and hold in back, k1, p1 from cn
	Sl 2 to cn and hold in front, p1, k2 from cn
	Sl 1 to cn and hold in back, k1, p1 from cn
	Sl 2 to cn and hold in front, k2, k2 from cn

Field of **Pansies**

Design by Mary J. Saunders

Basic stitches and an easy
pattern repeat form a light
and lacy afghan for baby.

Skill Level
Beginner*

Size
Approximately 38 x 38 inches

Materials
- Brown Sheep Handpaint Originals, 70 percent mohair/30 percent wool worsted weight yarn (88 yds/50g per hank): 8 hanks plum purple #HP45
- Size 11 (8mm) needles or size needed to obtain gauge

Gauge
10 sts and 16 rows = 4 inches/10cm in pat st
To save time, take time to check gauge.

Pattern Stitch
Pansy Pattern
Row 1: K6, *yo, k1, yo, k2tog, k1, k2tog, repeat from * to last 6 sts, k6.
Row 2: K6, *sl 1, k2tog, psso, yo, k3, yo, repeat from * to last 6 sts, k6.
Row 3: K6, *k2tog, k1, k2tog, yo, k1, yo, repeat from * to last 6 sts, k6.
Row 4: K6, *yo, k3, yo, sl 1, k2tog, psso, repeat from * to last 6 sts, k6.
Rep Rows 1–4 for pat.

Afghan
Cast on 96 sts.
Knit 12 rows.
Work even in pat until afghan measures approximately 36 inches, ending with Row 4.
Knit 12 rows.
Bind off.
Block lightly to measurements. ◆

April **Showers**

Design by Liliane Dickinson

Sunshine and showers, umbrellas and rainbows—
all show up in a whimsical child's afghan.

Skill Level
Intermediate***

Size
Appproximately 30 x 41 inches

Materials
- Brown Sheep Nature Spun, 100 percent wool worsted weight yarn (245 yds/100g per skein): 4 skeins meadow green #N56 (A), 2 skeins red fox #N46 (B), 2 skeins bit of blue #115 (C), 1 skein each sunburst gold #308 (D), orange you glad #N54 (E), amethyst #N62 (F), lullaby #307 (G), snow #740 (H), China blue #N36 (I)
- Size 13 (9mm) 29-inch circular needle
- Tapestry needle

Gauge
12 sts and 13 rows = 4 inches/10cm in color pat
To save time, take time to check gauge.

Pattern Notes
Afghan is worked with 2 strands of yarn held tog throughout.
Color pat is worked in St st from charts.
Edging is worked separately for each side, then sewn onto finished piece.
Umbrella Lace Edging st count changes from row to row.

Afghan
With B, cast on 65 sts.
Work color pat as follows:
Chart A: Work chart 8 times, rep first st once.

Chart B: Work chart 4 times, rep first st once.
Chart C: Work chart 16 times, rep first st once.
Chart D: Work chart 4 times, rep first st once.
Chart C: Work chart 16 times, rep first st once.
Chart E: Work rep 10 times, work to end of chart. Work for a total of 22 rows.
Rainbow Stripe: Work 2 rows each of colors F, I, A, G, E and B.
Chart F: Work chart twice, rep first st once.
Chart G: Work 5 sts with B, work chart, work 5 sts with B.
Chart H: Work rep 5 times, work to end of chart. Bind off in color pat.

Umbrella Lace Edging
(Multiple of 17 sts + 1)
Row 1 (RS): K1, *yo, k1, [p3, k1] 4 times, yo, rep from * across row.
Row 2 and all WS rows: Purl.
Row 3: K2, *yo, k1, [p3, k1] 4 times, yo, k2, rep from * across, end last rep k1.
Row 5: K3, *yo, k1, [p3, k1] 4 times, yo, k4, rep from * across, end last rep k2.
Row 7: K4, *yo, k1, [p2tog, p1, k1] 4 times, yo, k6, rep from * across, end last rep k3.
Row 9: K5, *yo, k1, [p2tog, k1] 4 times, yo, k8, rep from * across, end last rep k4.
Row 11: K6, *yo, k1, [k3tog, k1] 2 times, yo, k10, rep from * across, end last rep k5.

Side Borders
Make 2
With A, cast on 103 sts.
Work 11 rows of Umbrella Lace Edging.

Bind off purlwise on WS.

Top and Bottom Borders
Make 2
With A, cast on 69 sts.
Work 11 rows of Umbrella Lace Edging.

Bind off purlwise on WS.

Finishing
Sew side edgings to afghan first, then sew top and bottom edgings in place.
Block lightly. ◆

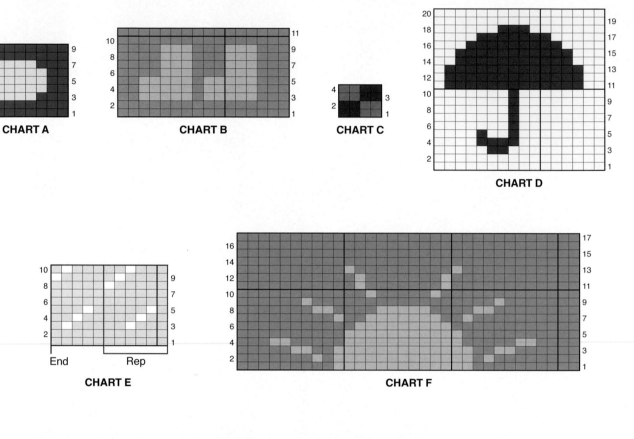

CHART A

CHART B

CHART C

CHART D

CHART E
End   Rep

CHART F

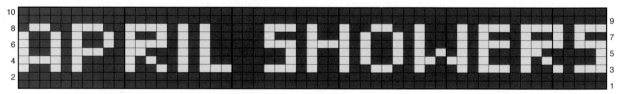

CHART G

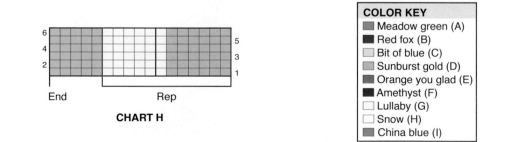

End   Rep
CHART H

COLOR KEY
- Meadow green (A)
- Red fox (B)
- Bit of blue (C)
- Sunburst gold (D)
- Orange you glad (E)
- Amethyst (F)
- Lullaby (G)
- Snow (H)
- China blue (I)

Star **Quilt**

Design by Nazanin S. Fard

This quiltlike afghan was inspired by the famous Ohio Star quilt pattern to create an heirloom piece.

Skill Level
Easy**

Size
Approximately 42 x 42 inches
Each block measures 8 inches

Materials
- Brown Sheep Top of the Lamb Sport, 100 percent wool sport weight yarn (350 yds/4 oz per hank) 15 hanks each red baron #420 and blanche #470, 10 hanks each appletree #403 and saffron #414, 5 hanks future purple #465
- Size 13 (9mm) needles
- Tapestry needle

Gauge
10 sts and 20 rows (10 ridges) = 4 inches/10cm in garter st with 5 strands of yarn held tog
To save time, take time to check gauge.

Special Abbreviation
Inc 1: K in front and back of same st.

Pattern Notes
This afghan is worked in blocks of garter st from point to point. The blocks are joined; the border is knit on last.
On single-color blocks, there is no change of color on Row 29.

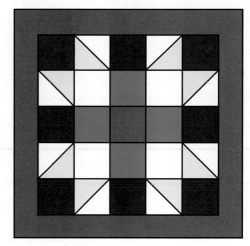

FIG. 1

COLOR KEY	
■	Red baron
□	Blanche
■	Apple tree
□	Saffron
■	Future purple

Block
(Make 1 future purple
4 apple tree
4 blanche
8 red baron
8 blanche/saffron)
With 5 strands of yarn held tog, cast on 3 sts.
Row 1 and all odd-numbered rows (RS): Knit.
Row 2: K1, inc 1, k1. (5 sts)
Row 4: K1, inc 1, k1, inc 1, k1. (7 sts)
Row 6: K1, inc 1, k3, inc 1, k1. (9 sts)
Row 8: K1, inc 1, k to last 2 sts, inc 1, k1. (11 sts)
Rep Row 8 until there are 31 sts. (If working two-color blocks, cut blanche and join saffron. Otherwise continue with same color yarn.)
Row 29: Knit.
Row 30 (beg decs): K1, ssk, k to last 3 sts, k2tog, k1. (29 sts)
Rep Row 30 until 5 sts remain.
Next row: K1, sl 1, k2tog, psso, k1.
Bind off.

Finishing
Sew blocks tog as shown in Fig. 1.

Border
With future purple, cast on 3 sts.
Row 1: K2, sl 1.
With RS facing, insert RH needle into corner st of afghan, pick up and k 1 st, psso, turn.
*Row 2: K3, turn.
Row 3: K2, sl 1, pick up and k 1 st in next ridge, psso, turn.
Rep Rows 2–3 until you reach next corner.
Work rows 1 and 2 in the same st to create a curved edge for the corner*, [rep from * to *] 3 times.
Rep Rows 1 and 2 again in first st.
Bind off 3 sts.
Sew ends of border tog. ◆

Bells & Lace

Design by Jacqueline Hoyle

A bell and bobble flounced
border grace the diagonal
lace center portion of a
traditional baby afghan.
The edges are finished
with I-cord.

Skill Level
Intermediate***

Size
Approximately 30 x 40 inches

Materials
- Brown Sheep Cotton Fleece, 80 percent cotton/20 percent Merino wool light worsted weight yarn (215 yards/100g per skein): 10 skeins cotton ball #CW100
- Size 10½ (6.5mm) 24-inch circular needle or size needed to obtain gauge
- Size K/10½ crochet hook
- Few yards smooth, bulky weight waste yarn
- Tapestry needle

Gauge
12 sts and 20 rows = 4 inches/10cm in Diagonal Madeira Lace pat
To save time, take time to check gauge.

Special Abbreviations
MB (make bobble): K in front, back, front, back, front of same st. Pass 2nd, 3rd, 4th and 5th sts over first st.
Provisional Cast On: With waste yarn and crochet hook, chain as directed. Fasten off. Turn chain over.
With working yarn, pick up and k 1 st in each bump on crochet chain. Yarn will be removed at end of project leaving live sts.

Pattern Stitches
A. Embossed Bell
Row 1 (RS): Purl.

Row 2: Knit.

Row 3: P6, *cast on 8 sts, p6, rep from * across.

Rows 4 and 6: K6, *p8, k6, rep from * across.

Row 5: P2, MB, p3, *k8, p2, MB, p3, rep from * across.

Row 7: P1, MB, p4, *ssk, k4, k2tog, p1, MB, p4, rep from * across.

Row 8: K6, *p6, k6, rep from * across.

Row 9: P3, MB, p2, *ssk, k2, k2tog, p3, MB, p2, rep from * across.

Row 10: K6, *p4, k6, rep from * across.

Row 11: P6, *ssk, k2tog, p6, rep from * across.

Row 12: K6, *p2, k6, rep from * across.

Row 13: P6, *k2tog, p6, rep from * across.

Row 14: K6, *p1, k6, rep from * across.

Row 15: P6, *k2tog, p5, rep from * across.

Row 16: Knit.

Rep Rows 1–16 for pat.

B. Diagonal Madeira Lace
(Multiple of 4 sts)

Row 1 and all other WS rows: Purl.

Row 2: K2, *yo, sl 1, k2tog, psso, yo, k1, rep from * across, end last rep k2.

Row 4: K2, *k1, yo, sl 1, k2tog, psso, yo, rep from * across, end last rep k2.

Row 6: K1, k2tog, *yo, k1, yo, sl 1, k2tog, psso, rep from * across, end last rep yo, k1, yo, ssk, k2.

Row 8: K2, k2tog, *yo, k1, yo, sl 1, k2tog, psso, rep from * across, end last rep yo, k1, yo, ssk, k1.

Rep Rows 1–8 for pat.

Pattern Notes
Two strands of yarn are held tog throughout.

Circular needle is used to accommodate all sts. Do not join; work in rows.

Yarn count changes on Embossed Bell pat. Original count will remain on Rows 1, 2, 15 and 16 only.

Afghan
With 2 strands of yarn held tog, cast on 108 sts using Provisional method.

Work 16 rows of Embossed Bell pat.

Knit 1 row, purl 1 row.

Set up pat (RS): Work Embossed Bell pat across 12 sts, pm, k84, pm, Embossed Bell pat on 12 sts.

Keeping sts between markers in Diagonal Madeira Lace pat, and 12 sts at each end in Embossed Bell pat, work even until afghan measures approximately 36 inches, ending with Row 16 of Embossed Bell pat.

Knit 1 row, purl 1 row.

Remove markers and work 16 rows of Embossed Bell pat across all sts.

Do not bind off, leave sts on needle.

I-Cord Border
Cast on 3 sts to LH needle.

K these 3 sts and slip them back to LH needle.

*K2 sts, k next st and 1 st from afghan tog-tbl, sl 3 sts back to LH needle. Rep from * across row until 1 afghan st remains, k3 sts without attaching, knit 1 attached row, k3 without attaching.

Slide 3 remaining sts to other end of needle*.

Using a double strand from a separate ball of yarn, pick up and k 3 sts for every 4 rows along side of afghan to next corner. Cut pick-up yarn.

Remove provisional cast on and place sts on needle next to ones just picked up, with separate ball of yarn, pick up and k 3 sts for every 4 rows along remaining edge, cut pick-up yarn.

Return to working yarn and [rep from * to *] 3 times as for first edge.

Weave remaining 3 sts to first cast-on sts of I-cord. Block lightly. ◆

Kid's Cabin Coverlet

Design by Katharine Hunt

This coverlet is worked using the entrelac method. The sophisticated colorway takes it from childhood through to college.

Skill Level
Advanced****

Size
Approximately 32 x 44 inches, lightly blocked

Materials
- Brown Sheep Lamb's Pride Superwash Worsted, 100 percent washable wool worsted weight yarn (200 yds/100g per ball): 3 balls each lichen #SW18 and midnight pine #SW63, 5 balls alabaster #SW10
- Size 10½ (6.5mm) 29-inch circular needles or size needed to obtain gauge
- Size J/10 crochet hook

Gauge
14 sts and 17 rows = 4 inches/10cm in St st lightly blocked
To save time, take time to check gauge.

Special Abbreviation
Ssp: Slip 1, p1, pass slipped st over

Pattern Notes
Circular needle is used to accommodate large number of sts. Do not join at end of row.
Coverlet is worked using 2 strands held tog throughout.
Color A is 1 strand each of lichen and midnight pine; color B is 2 strands of alabaster.
Coverlet is worked from side to side.
Border must fit short ends of coverlet, one point per adjacent triangle. If too wide, change to a size smaller needle.

Coverlet

1. Base Triangles
With A, cast on 84 sts.
Rows 1 and 2: P2, turn, k2, turn.
Rows 3 and 4: P3, turn, k3, turn.
Rows 5 and 6: P4, turn, k4, turn.
Rows 7 and 8: P5, turn, k5, turn.
Row 9: P6.
[Rep Rows 1–9] 13 more times. (14 triangles)
Cut A, join B.

2. Right Edge Triangle
Rows 1 (RS) and 2: K2, turn, p2, turn.
Rows 3 and 4: Inc by knitting into front and back of first st, ssk, turn, p3, turn.
Rows 5 and 6: Inc in first st, k1, ssk, turn, p4, turn.
Rows 7 and 8: Inc in first st, k2, ssk, turn, p5, turn.
Row 9: Inc in first st, k3, ssk, do not turn.

3. Left-Slanting Rectangle
With RS facing, pick up and k 6 sts down left side of adjacent triangle, turn.
Rows 1 and 2: P6, turn, k5, ssk (last B st and next A st), turn.
Rows 3–12: Rep Rows 1 and 2.
Rep Rows 1–12 until there are 13 rectangles.

4. Left Edge Triangle
Rows 1 and 2: With RS facing, pick up and k 6 sts along side of last triangle, turn, p2tog, p4, turn.
Rows 3 and 4: K5, turn, p2tog, p3, turn.
Rows 5 and 6: K4, turn, p2tog, p2, turn.

Rows 7 and 8: K3, turn, p2tog, p1, turn.
Rows 9 and 10: K2, turn, p2tog.
Cut B and draw through last st, leaving a 4-inch end to weave in.

5. Right-Slanting Rectangle
Rows 1 and 2: With A and WS facing, pick up and p 6 sts along side of edge triangle, turn, k6, turn.
Rows 3 and 4: P5, p2tog (last A st and next B st), turn, k6, turn.
Rows 5–12: Rep Rows 3 and 4.
Row 13: P5, p2tog. Do not turn.
Rep Rows 1–12 until there are 14 rectangles.
[Rep steps 2–5] 9 times more, [rep steps 2–4] once. Do not fasten off last st of left triangle.

Finishing Triangles
Rows 1 and 2: With A and WS facing, pick up and p 5 sts, turn, k6, turn.
Rows 3 and 4: P5, p2tog, turn, k6, turn.
Rows 5 and 6: P2tog, p3, p2tog, turn, k5, turn.
Rows 7 and 8: P2tog, p2, p2tog, turn, k4, turn.
Rows 9 and 10: P2tog, p1, p2tog, turn, k3, turn.
Rows 11 and 12: [P2tog] twice, turn, k2, turn.
Row 13: P3tog.
Rep Rows 1–13 until all sts are worked off.

Sawtooth Border
Make 2
With A, cast on 7 sts. Knit 2 rows.
Row 1 (RS): Yo, [k2tog, yo] twice, k3. (8 sts)
Row 2 and all WS rows: Knit.
Row 3: Yo, [K2tog, yo] twice, k4. (9 sts)
Row 5: Yo, [K2tog, yo] twice, k5. (10 sts)
Row 7: Yo, [K2tog, yo] twice, k6. (11 sts)
Row 9: Yo, [K2tog, yo] twice, k7. (12 sts)
Row 11: Yo, [K2tog, yo] twice, k8. (13 sts)
Row 12: Bind off 6 sts knitwise, k to end. (7 sts)
Rep Rows 1–12 until there are 11 points.
Knit 1 row.
Bind off knitwise.

Finishing
Pin coverlet to size, cover with damp cloth and leave overnight to dry.
With crochet hook and A, work 1 row sc along each short end of coverlet.
With RS facing, sew 1 border to each end, matching 1 point of border to each end triangle. ◆

This Way & That Way

Design by Barbara Venishnick

Garter stitch squares face in opposite directions to give an interesting look to this jewel of an afghan. It makes a great carry-along project.

Skill Level
Intermediate***

Size
Approximately 38 x 50 inches

Materials
- Brown Sheep Nature's Spectrum, 100 percent wool bulky weight yarn (81 yds/2 oz per hank): 14 hanks ocean treasures #W8300 (MC)
- Brown Sheep Handpaint Originals 70 percent mohair/30 percent wool worsted weight yarn (88 yds/50g hanks): 6 hanks peacock #HP65 (CC)
- Size 11 (8mm) straight, 2 double-pointed and (2) 29-inch circular needles or size needed to obtain gauge
- Size J/10 crochet hook

Gauge
10 sts and 20 rows (10 ridges) = 4 inches/10cm in garter st with MC
To save time, take time to check gauge.

Pattern Note
Afghan is made in garter st squares; squares are joined with three-needle bind off.

Squares
Make 48
With MC, cast on 18 stitches.
Every row: K1-tbl, k16, sl 1 wyif.
[Rep this row] 31 times. (16 ridges)
Bind off.

Joining Squares
Afghan is organized into 6 rows of 8 squares each.
With 2 strands of CC held tog and dpn, pick up and k 16 sts along bound-off edge of first square. Do not cut yarn. Continuing with same double strand of yarn and 2nd dpn, pick up and k 16 sts along side edge of 2nd square.
Fold 2nd square behind first, having WS tog and needles parallel.
Working end of yarn will be at the right of work; 'folded' end of picked-up sts will be at the left.
Keeping working yarn between needles at all times, work three-needle bind off as follows:
*Insert RH needle into first st of front square knitwise, then into first st of back square purlwise, wrap yarn around needle and pull through both sts, sl both sts off needles. Rep from * once (2 sts on RH needle). Pass first st over 2nd st as in regular bind off. Continue to work in this manner until all sts are bound off. Cut yarn and fasten off final st.
A flat knit chain has been created between first and 2nd squares.
Continue to join squares in same manner, alternating directions of ridges by joining selvage edges to cast-on or bound-off edges until you have a long strip of 8 squares. Make 5 more strips, making sure

Continued on page 47

Blue**bells**

Design by Lois S. Young

The motifs in this easy lace pattern resemble bluebells.
If you turn it upside down, you will see tulips.

Skill Level
Easy**

Size
Approximately 33 x 38 inches

Materials
- Brown Sheep Top of the Lamb, 100 percent wool worsted weight yarn (190 yds/4 oz per skein): 4 skeins sky blue #170
- Size 10½ (6.5mm) needles or size needed to obtain gauge

Gauge
11 sts and 18 rows = 4 inches/10cm in pat st after blocking
To save time, take time to check gauge.

Special Abbreviation
CDD (centered double decrease): Sl 2 sts tog knitwise, k2, pass 2 sl sts over.

Pattern Notes
Sl first st of each row knitwise.
Lace must be blocked severely. Dampen blanket and pin out on sheet or bedspread on floor. Let dry.

Blanket
Loosely cast on 97 sts.
Knit 6 rows.
Beg chart, working rep between red lines 8 times.
[Work 8-row rep] 20 times, rep Rows 1 - 7.
Knit 7 rows.
Bind off knitwise on WS.
Block to measurements. ◆

Rep

BLUEBELLS CHART

STITCH KEY
- ☐ K on RS, p on WS
- ⊟ P on RS, k on WS
- ⅄ CDD
- ◺ Ssk
- ◹ K2tog
- ○ Yo
- ∩ Sl 1

Lace Blocks

Design by Diane Zangl

The unique combination of large needles and worsted weight yarn join to produce a light and lacy baby blanket, finished with a dainty crochet edging. The decreases and yarn overs produce squares that are at an angle.

Skill Level
Intermediate***

Size
Approximately 42 x 42 inches after blocking

Materials
- Brown Sheep Cotton Fleece, 80 percent cotton/20 percent Merino wool light worsted weight yarn (215 yds/100g per skein): 5 skeins nymph #CW610
- Size 10½ (6.5mm) 24-inch circular needles or size needed to obtain gauge
- Size H/8 (5mm) crochet hook
- Tapestry needle

Gauge
14 sts and 22 rows = 4 inches/10cm in pat
To save time, take time to check gauge.

Pattern Note
Circular needles are used to accommodate large amount of sts. Do not join; work back and forth in rows.

Blanket
Cast on 140 sts. Purl 1 row.
Set up pat: K2, referring to chart [work from A–B] 8 times, [work from B–C] once, k2.
Work even, keeping first and last 2 sts in St st and rem sts in established pat.
[Rep Rows 1–24] 9 times, [rep Rows 1–12] once.
Knit 1 row.

Bind off. Do not cut yarn. Sl last st to crochet hook.

Edging
Work 1 rnd sc around blanket, making sure to keep work flat. Join with sl st.
Rnd 2: *Ch 2, sl st in next sc, rep from * around. Join with sl st, fasten off.
Block. ◆

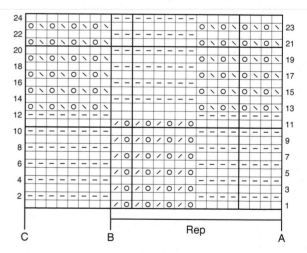

LACE BLOCKS CHART

STITCH KEY
- ☐ K on RS, p on WS
- ⊟ P on RS, k on WS
- ⊙ Yo
- ⟋ K2tog
- ⟍ Ssk

Baby **Blocks**

Design by Kennita Tully

Blocks of diamond and square motifs
embellish an afghan knit in ocean colors.

Skill Level
Easy**

Size
Approximately 32 x 35 inches

Materials
- Brown Sheep Cotton Fleece, 80 percent cotton/20 percent Merino wool light worsted weight yarn (215 yds/100g per skein): 4 skeins each dusty sage #CW380 (A) and rue #CW375 (B), 2 skeins lilac haze #CW695 (C)
- Size 17 (12mm) 29-inch circular needles or size needed to obtain gauge

Gauge
7 sts and 11 rows = 4 inches/10cm in Seed st
To save time, take time to check gauge.

Pattern Stitches
A. Seed Stitch
All Rows: K1, *p1, k1, rep from * across row.
B. Block Patterns
Diamond A
Rows 1 and 3: Knit.
Row 2: Purl.
Row 4: P6, k1, p6.
Row 5: K5, p1, k1, p1, k5.
Row 6: P4, [k1, p1] twice, k1, p4.
Row 7: K3, [p1, k1] 3 times, p1, k3.
Row 8: P2, [k1, p1] 4 times, k1, p2.
Row 9: K1, *p1, k1, rep from * across row.
Row 10: Rep Row 8.
Row 11: Rep Row 7.
Row 12: Rep Row 6.

Row 13: Rep Row 5.
Row 14: Rep Row 4.
Rows 15 and 17: Knit.
Row 16: Purl.
Square A
Rows 1 and 3: Knit.
Row 2: Purl.
Rows 4, 6, 8, 10, 12 and 14: P3, [k1, p1] 3 times, k1, p3.
Rows 5, 7, 9, 11 and 13: K4, [p1, k1] twice, p1, k4.
Rows 15 and 17: Knit.
Row 16: Purl.
Diamond B
Rows 1 and 3: Purl.
Row 2: Knit.
Row 4: K6, p1, k6.
Row 5: P5, k1, p1, k1, p5.
Row 6: K4, [p1, k1] twice, p1, p4.
Row 7: P3, [k1, p1] 3 times, k1, p3.
Row 8: K2, [p1, k1] 4 times, p1, k2.
Row 9: P1, *k1, p1 rep from * across row.
Row 10: Rep Row 8.
Row 11: Rep Row 7.
Row 12: Rep Row 6.
Row 13: Rep Row 5.
Row 14: Rep Row 4.
Rows 15 and 17: Purl.
Row 16: Knit.
Square B
Rows 1 and 3: Purl.
Row 2: Knit.
Rows 4, 6, 8, 10, 12 and 14: K3, [p1, k1] 3 times, p1, k3.

Continued on page 47

Rio Grande Stripes

Design by E.J. Slayton

Beginning with the sheep that came into New Mexico with Coronado in 1540, wool and weaving have played an important part in the culture of the American Southwest. This afghan is based on woven blankets from the mid-1800s, worked in an easy pattern of garter, stockinette and simple slip-stitch stripes.

Skill Level
Easy**

Size
Approximately 38 x 54 (43 x 66) inches
Instructions are given for smaller size, with larger size in parentheses. When only 1 number is given, it applies to both sizes.

Materials
- Brown Sheep Burly Spun, 100 percent wool super-bulky weight yarn (132 yds/8 oz per hank): 4 (5) hanks black #BS05 (MC), 2 (3) hanks limeade #BS120 (A), 1 (2) hanks orange you glad #BS110 (B), 1 hank periwinkle #BS59 (C)
- Size 13 (9mm) needles or size needed to obtain gauge
- Tapestry needle

Gauge
9 sts and 12 rows = 4 inches/10cm in St st
To save time, take time to check gauge.

Pattern Stitches
A. Wide Stripe (uneven number of sts)
Row 1 (RS): With A, k5, *sl 1, k1, rep from * to last 4 sts, end k4.
Row 2: With A, sl 1, k3, p1, *sl 1, p1, rep from * to last 4 sts, end k3, sl 1.
Row 3: With A, knit.
Row 4: With A, sl 1, k3, p to last 4 sts, end k3, sl 1.
Row 5: With B, k5, *sl 1, k1, rep from * to last 4 sts, end k4.
Row 6: With B, sl 1, k4, *sl 1, k1, rep from * to last 4 sts, end k3, sl 1.
Row 7: With B, knit.
Row 8: With B, sl 1, k to last st, end sl 1.
Rows 9–12: Rep Rows 1–4.
Row 13: With MC, k4, *sl 1, k1, rep from * to last 5 sts, end sl 1, k4.
Row 14: With MC, sl 1, k3, *sl 1, p1, rep from * to last 5 sts, end sl 1, k3, sl 1.
B. Narrow Stripe (multiple of 4 sts + 1)
Row 1 (RS): With C, knit.
Row 2: With C, sl 1, k to last st, sl 1.

Row 3: With A, k4, *sl 1, k3, rep from * to last 5 sts, end sl 1, k4.
Row 4: With A, *sl 1, k3, rep from * to last st, sl 1.
Rows 5 and 6: With C, rep Rows 1 and 2.

Pattern Notes

Sl all sts purlwise with yarn on WS of fabric.
Sl first and last st of all WS rows.
When working sl st stripes, be careful not to pull yarn too tightly behind sl sts.
Except in Narrow Stripe, break color not in use and re-attach next time it is needed.

Afghan

With A, cast on 77 (87) sts.
Row 1 (WS): Sl 1, k to last st, sl 1.
Row 2: Knit.
Rows 3 and 4: Rep Rows 1 and 2.
Row 5: Rep Row 1.

Knit, inc 8 (10) sts evenly. (85, 97 sts)
Next row: Sl 1, k3, p to last 4 sts, k3, sl 1.
Work Rows 5–14 of Wide Stripe, then work 10 rows MC.
Work Narrow Stripe, then work 12 rows MC.
Work Rows 1–14 of Wide Stripe, then work 32 rows MC. Rep Narrow Stripe.
For larger size only: Work 12 rows MC, Rows 1–14 of Wide Stripe, 12 rows MC, rep Narrow Stripe.
Both sizes: Work 32 rows MC, Rows 1–14 of Wide Stripe, 12 rows MC, Narrow Stripe, 12 rows MC, rep Rows 1–12 of Wide Stripe.
Next row: With A knit, dec 8 (10) sts evenly. (77, 87 sts)
Knit 4 rows, sl first and last sts of WS rows.
Bind off knitwise on WS.
Block. ◆

Little Gems
Continued from page 18

Row 2: K1, inc 1 by knitting into front and back of next st, k to last 2 sts, inc 1 in next st, k1.
Rows 3–8: Rep Rows 1 and 2, using color C on Rows 4 and 5.
Bind off on WS knitwise.
Rep border along cast-on edge.
Work side borders the same, picking up and k 156 sts instead of 117.
Sew corners tog. ◆

Heart of Mine
Continued from page 20

Afghan

Holding 3 strands tog, cast on 96 sts.
Knit 4 rows.
Set up pat (WS): Garter st over 3 sts, pm, work Row 1 of [Irish Moss pat over 10 sts, Back Cable pat over 8 sts] twice, pm, Cabled Heart pat from chart over 18 sts, pm, [Front Cable pat over 8 sts, Irish Moss pat over 10 sts] twice, pm, garter st over 3 sts.
Work even in established pats until 8 heart pats have been completed.
Knit 4 rows.
Bind off. ◆

This Way & That Way
Continued from page 36

that 3 strips have beginning squares facing in opposite directions as others.

Joining Strips
Hold first strip with RS facing, using double strand of CC and circular needle, pick up and k 16 sts in each square along right edge of strip. Cut yarn.
With 2nd circular needle pick up and k 16 sts in each square along left edge of 2nd strip. Hold strips with WS tog, making sure squares form a 'checker board' pat. Join strips with three-needle bind off as for individual squares.

Join remaining strips to those previously finished.

Edging
With double strand of CC, work 16 sc in each square along outside edge of afghan, working 2 sc in each corner st and making sure to keep work flat. Join with sl st. Block. ◆

Baby Blocks
Continued from page 42

Rows 5, 7, 9, 11 and 13: P4, [k1, p1] twice, k1, p4.
Rows 15 and 17: Purl.
Row 16: Knit.

Pattern Notes
Five strands of yarn are held tog for entire afghan: 2 strands each of A and B, and 1 strand C. Borders and motifs are worked in Seed st.

Blanket
With 5 strands of yarn held tog, cast on 57 sts.
Work in Seed st for 6 rows.
*Next Row (RS): Work Seed st over 5 sts, Diamond A over 13 sts, Seed st over 4 sts, Square A over 13 sts, Seed st over 4 sts, Diamond A over 13 sts, Seed st over 5 sts.
Work even in established pat for 16 more rows.

Work 6 rows of Seed st.
Next Row (WS):
Work Seed st over 5 sts, Square B over 13 sts, Seed st over 4 sts, Diamond B over 13 sts, Seed st over 4 sts, Square B over 13 sts, Seed st over 5 sts.
Work even in established pat for 16 more rows.
Work 6 rows of Seed st.
Rep from * once.
Bind off.
Block blanket to finished measurements. ◆

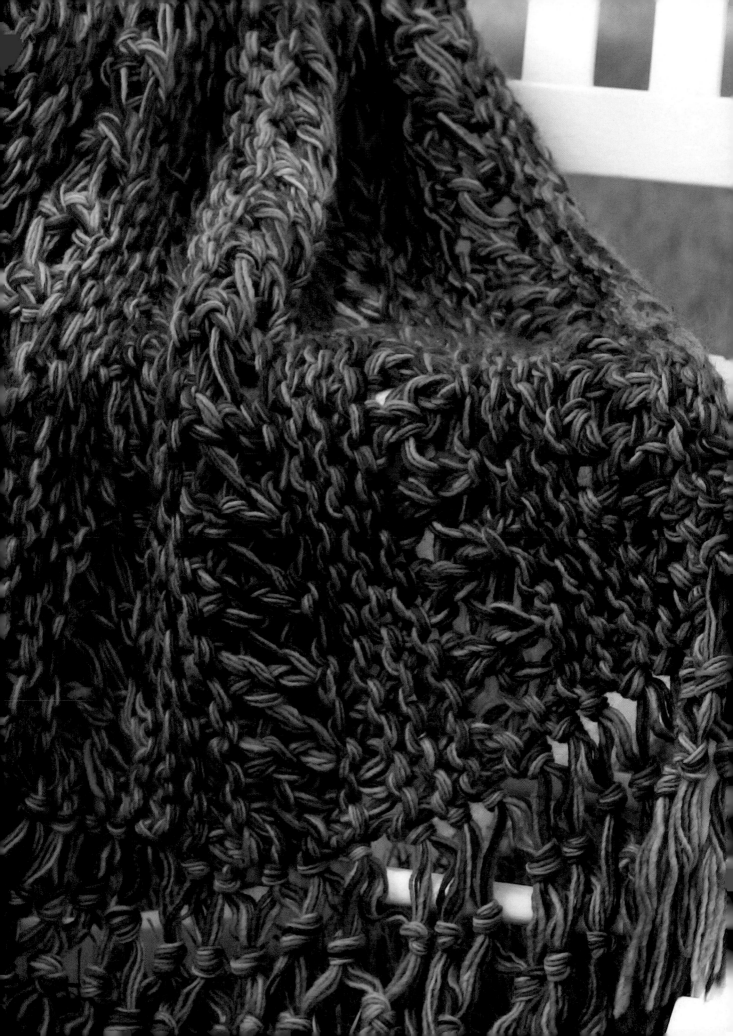

COZY **COMFORTS**

Summer **Meadow**

Design by Susan Robicheau

Slip stitches along with an easily memorized pattern combined in an afghan that reminds one of a meadow of flowers.

Skill Level
Easy**

Size
Approximately 49 x 64 inches

Materials
- Brown Sheep Nature Spun, 100 percent wool worsted weight yarn (245 yds/100g per skein): 6 skeins monument green #N27 (B), 4 skeins each pink please #N98 (A), Victorian pink #N87 (C) and natural #730 (D)
- Size 11 (8mm) 32-inch circular needle or size needed to obtain gauge
- Size J/10 crochet hook
- Tapestry needle

Gauge
14 sts and 20 rows = 4 inches/10cm in Meadow pat with 2 strands held tog
To save time, take time to check gauge.

Pattern Stitch
Meadow
Row 1 (WS): With A k1, p to last st, k1.
Row 2: With B k2, *sl 1 wyib, k1, rep from * to last st, k1.
Row 3: With B k1, p1, *sl 1 wyif, p1, rep from * to last st, k1.
Row 4: With C k1, *sl 1 wyib, k1, rep from * across row.
Row 5: With C k1, p to last st, k1.
Row 6: With D k1, *sl 1 wyib, k3, rep from * to last 2 sts, sl 1 wyib, k1.
Row 7: With D k1, *sl 1 wyif, p3, rep from * to last 2 sts, sl 1 wyif, k1.
Row 8: With B k2, *sl 3 wyib, k1, rep from * to last st, k1.
Row 9: With B k1, p2, *sl 1 wyif, p3, rep from * to last 4 sts, sl 1 wyif, p2, k1.
Row 10: With A k1, *sl 1 wyib, k3, rep from * to last 2 sts, sl 1 wyib, k1.
Rep Rows 1–10 for pat.

Pattern Notes
Two strands of yarn are held tog for entire afghan. Circular needle is used to accommodate large number of sts. Do not join; work in rows.

Afghan
With A, cast on 163 sts.
Work even in Meadow pat until afghan measures approximately 60 inches, ending with Row 10 of pat.
Bind off.

Side Border
With B, pick up and k 161 sts along one side of afghan.
Row 1 (WS): K1, p to last st, k1.
Row 2: K1, *p3, sl 1 wyib, rep from * to last st, k1.
Row 3: K1, *k3, p1, rep from * to last st, k1.

Continued on page 88

Lavender **Mist**

Design by Carolyn Pfeifer

An easy yarn-over pattern combines with superwash yarn in an afghan that will be used by young and old alike.

Skill Level
Beginner*

Size
Approximately 47 x 59 inches

Materials
- Brown Sheep Lamb's Pride Superwash Bulky, 100 percent washable wool bulky weight yarn (110 yds/100g per skein) 14 skeins mountain lavender #SW140
- Size 10½ (6.5mm) 29-inch circular knitting needle or size needed to obtain gauge
- Size H/8 crochet hook

Gauge
21 sts and 15 rows = 4 inches/10cm in pat st
To save time, take time to check gauge.

Pattern Stitch
Lavender Mist
Row 1: *K1, p1; rep from * across row.
Row 2 and all even-numbered rows: Purl.
Row 3: *P1, k1; rep from * across row.
Row 5: Rep Row 1.
Row 7: K2, *ssk, yo, k1, yo, k2tog, k1; rep from * across, end last rep k2.
Row 9: K1,*yo, sl 1, k2tog, psso, yo, k2; rep from * across, end last rep k3.

Row 11: K2, *yo, sl 1, k2tog, yo, k2; rep from * across, end last rep k2.
Row 13: Rep Row 9.
Row 15: Rep Row 7.
Row 16: Purl.
Rep Rows 1–16 for pat.

Pattern Note
Circular needles are used to accommodate large number of sts. Do not join; work in rows.

Afghan
Cast on 152 sts.
Work even in pat st until afghan measures approximately 59 inches, ending with Row 6 of pat.
Bind off knitwise on RS.

Edging
Work 1 rnd sc around entire afghan, working 2 sc at each corner and making sure to keep work flat.

Fringe
Cut strands of yarn, each 6 inches long.
Fold 3 strands tog and knot through every other st along top and bottom edges.
Trim fringe even. ◆

Jewel Tones

Design by Janet Rehfeldt

Jewel-like colors and a luxurious triple fringe
highlight an afghan fit for a queen.

Skill Level
Easy**

Size
Approximately 50 x 64 inches, without fringe

Materials
- Brown Sheep Lamb's Pride Worsted, 85 percent wool/15 percent mohair worsted weight yarn (190 yds/4 oz per skein): 6 skeins each periwinkle #M59, RPM pink #M105, sunburst gold #M14, Aztec turquoise #M78
- Brown Sheep Handpaint Originals 70 percent mohair/30 percent wool worsted weight yarn (88 yds/50g per skein): 11 skeins tropical waters #HP60
- Size 35 (20mm) 47-inch circular needle or size needed to obtain gauge

Gauge
6 sts and 8 rows = 4 inches/10cm in garter st
To save time, take time to check gauge.

Pattern Stitch
Rows 1 (RS)–6: K2, *yo, k2tog; rep from * across, end last rep k2.
Rows 7–14: Knit.
Rep Rows 1–4 for pat.

Pattern Notes
Afghan is worked with 5 strands of yarn (one of each color) held tog throughout.
Circular needle is used to accommodate large number of stitches. Do not join; work in rows.

Afghan
Cast on 94 sts.
Beg with a RS row, knit 4 rows.
Work even in pat until afghan measures approximately 47 inches, ending with Row 6 of pat.
Knit 3 rows.
Bind off knitwise on WS.

Triple Knot Fringe
Cut strands into 35-inch lengths.
Using 5 strands held tog (1 of each color), fold strands in half.
Knot 1 group of strands in each row along edge of afghan.
Take half of strands from first group, and knot them tog with half of strands of adjoining group about 1½ inches below first knots. Rep across row.
Beg with free half of first group, make a 3rd row of knots about 1½ inches below previous ones.
Trim ends even.
Rep for opposite edge of afghan. ◆

Bamboo **Fence**

Design by Barbara Venishnick

Natural shades and rugged texture are used in an afghan that will coordinate beatifully with den decor.

Skill Level
Easy**

Size
Approximately 62 x 46 inches

Materials
- Brown Sheep Lamb's Pride Worsted, 85 percent wool/15 percent mohair worsted weight yarn (190 yds/4 oz per hank): 4 hanks each crème #M10 (A), wild oak #M08 (B), sable #M07 (C) and charcoal heather #M04 (D)
- Size 11 (8mm) 29-inch circular needle or size needed to obtain gauge

Gauge
10 sts and 14 rows = 4 inches/10cm in St st with double strand of yarn
To save time, take time to check gauge.

Pattern Notes
Two strands of yarn are held tog for entire afghan.
Circular needles are used to accommodate large number of sts. Do not join, work in rows.
On all rows except 9 and 10, leave an 8-inch tail of beginning and ending color. This will be used later for fringe.
Wind separate bobbins for each of the color A vertical bars. Carry other color in use behind the 4-st bar.

Afghan
With A, cast on 164 sts.
Row 1 (WS): [P38 B, p4 A] 3 times, p38 B.
Rows 2, 4, 6 and 8: [P38 B, k4 A] 3 times, p38 B.
Rows 3, 5 and 7: [K38 B, p4 A] 3 times, k38 B.
Row 9: With A, purl.
Row 10: With A, knit.
Rows 11–18: Rep Rows 1–8, using color C instead of B.
Rows 19 and 20: Rep Rows 9 and 10.
Rows 21–28: Rep Rows 1–8, using color D instead of B.
Rows 29 and 30: Rep Rows 9 and 10.
[Rep Rows 1–30] 5 times more, ending with Row 29.
Bind off all sts purlwise.

Fringe
Gather long ends of colors at end of each color band and pull them tightly to straighten edges of knitting.
Tie an overhand knot with each group of colors, tightening knot as close to afghan as possible.
Trim fringe even. ◆

Dotted **Stripes**

Design by Lois S. Young

This colorway is mindful of spring flowers and would make a charming accent in a girl's room.

Skill Level
Easy**

Size
Approximately 44 x 66 inches

Materials
- Brown Sheep Cotton Fleece, 80 percent cotton/20 percent Merino wool light worsted weight yarn (215 yds/100g per skein): 14 skeins cotton ball #CW100 (MC), 2 skeins each lime light CW840 (A) and tea rose CW210 (B)
- Size 13 (9mm) 36-inch circular needle or size needed to obtain gauge

Gauge
10 sts and 14 rows = 4 inches/10cm in Picot Stripes pat
To save time, take time to check gauge.

Special Abbreviations
Ssp: Sl 2 sts separately knitwise, return sts to LH needle in this reversed position, p2tog through back of sts.
Picot: (K1, [yo, k1] 3 times) in next st, making 7 sts out of 1.

Pattern Stitches
A. Seed Stitch
All rows: *K1, p1; rep from * across, end last rep k1.
B. Picot Stripes
Row 1 (WS): With MC, k1, p to last st, k1.
Row 2: With A k3, *picot, k9; rep from * across, end last rep picot, k3.
Row 3: With A knit.
Row 4: With MC, k2 *k2tog, k5, ssk, k7; rep from * across, end last rep k2tog, k5, ssk, k2.
Row 5: K1, p1, *ssp, p1, sl 1 wyif, p1, p2tog, p7; rep from * across, end last rep p1, k1.
Row 6: K2, *k2tog, sl 1 wyib, ssk, k7; rep from * across, end last rep k2.
Row 7: K1, p to last st, k1.
Row 8: With B, k8, *picot, k9; rep from * across, end last rep picot, k8.
Row 9: With B, knit.
Row 10: With MC, k7, *k2tog, k5, ssk, k7; rep from * across row.
Row 11: K1 , p6, *ssp, p1, sl 1 wyif, p1, p2tog, p7; rep from * across, end last rep p6, k1.
Row 12: K7, *k2tog, sl 1 wyib, ssk, k7; rep from * across row.
Rows 13–18: Rep Rows 1–6.
Rows 19–38: Work in St st, keeping first and last st in k.
Rows 39–76: Rep Rows 1–38, working color stripe sequence as B, A, B.

Pattern Notes
Afghan is worked with 3 strands of yarn held tog throughout.
Circular needle is used to accommodate large number of sts. Do not join, work in rows.

Afghan
With MC, cast on 87 sts loosely.
Work in Seed St for 6 rows.
Knit 1 row.
Next row: P1, k to last st, p1.
[Work Picot Stripe pat] 3 times.

Continued on page 89

Wrapped in **Ripples**

Design by Lois S. Young

Here is a knit variation of the favorite crochet ripple afghan.

Skill Level
Easy**

Size
Approximately 43 x 53 inches

Materials
- Brown Sheep Lamb's Pride Worsted, 85 percent wool/15 percent mohair worsted weight yarn (190 yds/4 oz per skein): 4 skeins blue flannel #M82 (A), 3 skeins each white frost #M11 (B), lotus pink #M38 (C) and blue boy #M79 (D)
- Size 13 (9mm) 32-inch circular needle or size needed to obtain gauge

Gauge
17 stitches and 8 rows = 4 inches/10cm in pat
To save time, take time to check gauge.

Pattern Stitch
Ripples
Row 1 (RS): Sl 1, k1, *(k1, [yo, k1] twice) in same st, [ssk] 3 times, sl 2, k1, p2sso, [k2tog] 3 times, (k1, [yo, k1] twice) in same st; rep from * across, end last rep k2.
Row 2: Sl 1, k1, p to last 2 sts, k2.
Rep Rows 1–2 for pat.

Pattern Notes
Two strands of yarn are held tog for entire afghan.
Circular needle is used to accommodate large number of stitches. Do not join; work in rows.
Slip first st of each row knitwise.
Color sequence: Work 2 rows each of B, C, D and A.

Afghan
With A, cast on 191 sts loosely.
Work Rows 1 and 2 of Ripples pat, rep Row 1.
Next row: Sl 1, k to end of row.
Work in color sequence for 13 reps, ending with Row 1 of color A.
Next row: Sl 1, k to end of row.
Rep Row 1.
Bind off knitwise on WS.

Side Border
With RS facing, pick up and k 1 st in each row along side edge.
Knit 2 rows, slipping first st of each row knitwise.
Bind off knitwise on WS.
Rep border along 2nd edge.
Block, pinning out points at both ends. ◆

Sporty Squares

Design by Katharine Hunt

Cables and color mix together for a sporty afghan. Make one in your favorite team colors.

Skill Level
Intermediate***

Size
Approximately 42 x 59 inches, lightly blocked

Materials
- Brown Sheep Burly Spun, 100 percent wool super-bulky weight yarn (132 yds/8 oz per hank): 7 hanks prairie fire #BS181 (MC), 4 hanks oatmeal #BS115 (CC)
- Size 15 (10mm) needles or size needed to obtain gauge

Gauge
10 sts and 17 rows = 4 inches/10cm in Bicolor pat
To save time, take time to check gauge.

Pattern Notes
Afghan is worked in 5 panels of 7 squares each.
Slip all sts purlwise.
Solid Squares are worked in either MC or CC.
MC squares are used alternately with all others in each panel.
When working Bicolor Square: On Rows 1 and 5, wrap color not in use loosely over working strand before purling last st, to position it for color change on next row.

Solid Square
Setup pat: With color indicated,
For first square in a panel only: Beg with a RS row, knit 3 rows.
For 2nd–7th squares in a panel: Purl 2 rows, beg with a WS row.

Begin pat
Row 1 (WS): Purl.
Row 2: P1, k1, p1, *sl 1 wyib, k1, sl 1 wyib, p1; rep from * across, end last rep k1, p1.
Row 3: P5, *sl 1 wyif, p3; rep from * across row.
Row 4: P1, k1, *p1, drop sl st off needle to front of work, k2, pick up dropped st and knit it; rep from * across, end last rep p1, k1, p1.
[Rep Rows 1–4] 6 times.
Knit 2 rows.
Final square only: Bind off knitwise on WS.

Bicolor Square
Setup pat: With CC,
For first square in panel only: With CC, beg with a RS row, knit 3 rows, purl 1 row, knit 1 row.
For 2nd–7th squares in a panel: With CC, beg with a WS row, purl 3 rows, knit 1 row.

Begin pat
Row 1 (WS): With CC, purl.
Row 2: With MC, p1, k2, *sl 1 wyib, k1; rep from * across, end last rep sl 1 wyib, k2, p1.
Row 3: With MC, p5, *sl 1 wyif, p3; rep from * across row.
Row 4: With MC, p1, k2, *drop sl st off needle to front of work, k2, pick up dropped st and knit it, k1; rep from * across, end last rep k1, p1.
Row 5: With MC, purl.
Rows 6–8: With CC, rep Rows 2–4.
[Rep Rows 1–8] twice.
With CC, purl 1 row, knit 3 rows.
Final square only: Bind off knitwise on WS.

Continued on page 89

Wings & Waves

Design by Katharine Hunt

Long, slanting stitches give the appearance of birds hovering over ocean waves.

Skill Level
Advanced****

Size
Approximately 44 x 57 inches after light blocking

Materials
• Brown Sheep Nature Spun, 100 percent wool worsted weight yarn (245 yds/100g per skein): 10 skeins bit of blue #115 (A), 6 skeins natural #730 (B)
• Size 10½ (6.5mm) 29-inch circular needle
• Size 11 (8mm) 29-inch circular needle or size needed to obtain gauge
• Stitch holders

Gauge
15 sts and 24 rows = 4 inches/10cm in pat st with larger needles
To save time, take time to check gauge.

Pattern Stitch
Wings & Waves
(Multiple of 8 sts + 2)
Row 1 (WS): With A, k4, *p2 wrapping yarn twice for each st, k6; rep from * across, end last rep k4.
Row 2: With B, k4, *sl 2 wyib dropping extra wraps, k6; rep from * across, end last rep k4.
Row 3: With B, k4, *sl 2 wyif, k6; rep from * across, end last rep k4.
Row 4: With B, k4, *sl 2 wyib, k6; rep from * across, end last rep k4.
Row 5: With B, k3, *p1 wrapping yarn twice, sl 2 wyif, p1 wrapping yarn twice, k4; rep from * across, end last rep k3.
Row 6: With A k1, *sl 3 wyib dropping extra wrap from 3rd st; drop first long color-A st off needle to front of work, sl same 3 sts back to LH needle,

pick up dropped st and knit it; then k2, sl 1 wyib, drop 2nd long color-A st off needle to front of work, sl 3 wyib dropping extra wrap from first st, pick up dropped st and place on LH needle, then sl2 (the 2nd and 3rd sts) of the 3 slipped sts back to LH needle, k3; rep from * across, end last rep k1.

Rows 7–10: Rep Rows 3–6, reversing colors (i.e., A, A, A, B).

Rep Rows 3–10 for pat.

Pattern Notes

Afghan is worked using 2 same-color strands tog throughout.

Take care not to twist long sts when replacing on needle.

Carry color not in use loosely up side of work, catching in on each RS row.

Sl sts purlwise.

Afghan

With smaller needle and 2 strands of A held tog, cast on 168 sts.

Knit 9 rows.

Next row (WS): K7, sl these sts to holder and leave at side of work.

Change to larger needle.

**With A, work Row 1 of Wings & Waves pat to last 7 sts.

Sl 7 sts to holder and leave at side of work.

Beg with Row 2, continue in established pat on center sts only, [working Rows 3–10] 6 times, rep Rows 3 and 4.

Separating Bands

Row 1 (WS): With B, *k4, sl 2 wyif, k2; rep from * across, end last rep k2.

Row 2: With A k1, *sl 3 purlwise wyib, drop first long color-A st off needle to front of work, sl the same 3 sts back to LH needle, pick up dropped st and knit it; k3. Drop second long color-A st off needle to front of work, sl 3 wyib, pick up dropped st and place on LH needle, then sl 3 slipped sts back to LH needle, k4; rep from * across, end last rep k1.

Change to smaller needle.

With A, knit 3 rows.

With B, knit 2 rows.

With A, knit 3 rows.**

Change to larger needle and rep from ** to ** 3 times.

[Work Rows 3–7 of Wings & Waves pat] 6 times.

Rep Rows 3 and 4.

Work Rows 1 and 2 of separating band.

Leave sts on needle and set aside.

Side Borders

Sl sts from holder at right edge of afghan to smaller needle.

Join A. Starting with a WS row, work in garter st until border, slightly stretched, matches length of afghan, ending with a WS row. Do not bind off, sl sts to holder.

With RS facing, sew border to afghan to within a few inches of top edge. Add or subtract rows, if necessary, to match afghan length. Sew remaining seam.

Sl border sts to end of afghan needle.

Rep for left border.

Top Border

Change to smaller needle.

With A, knit across all sts, including side borders.

Knit 8 more rows.

Bind off knitwise on WS.

Fringe

Cut 6 strands of yarn, each 10 inches long.

Fold strands in half and knot into cast-on edge of afghan, positioning each group of fringe at point of pat.

Rep fringe along bound-off edge. ◆

Crisscross Diamonds

Design by Katharine Hunt

Add a touch of the Aran Islands with a classic throw in natural cream color.

Skill Level
Intermediate***

Size
Approximately 46 x 58 inches, lightly blocked

Materials
- Brown Sheep Lamb's Pride Superwash Bulky, 100 percent washable wool bulky weight yarn (110 yds/100g per skein): 19 skeins alabaster #SW10
- Size 10 (6mm) 29-inch circular needle
- Size 10½ (6.5mm) 29-inch circular needle or size needed to obtain gauge
- Cable needle
- Stitch holders

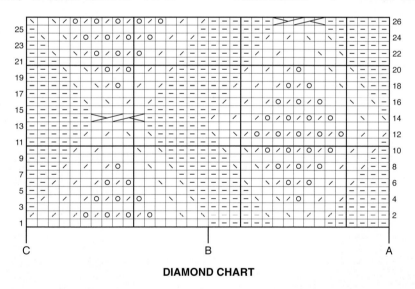

DIAMOND CHART

STITCH KEY
☐ K on RS, p on WS
⊟ P on RS, k on WS
⊙ Yo
⟋ K2tog
⟋⟋ Sl 1 to cn and hold in back, k2, k1 from cn
⟍⟍ Sl 2 to cn and hold in front. k1, k2 from cn
⟍⟋ Sl 3 sts to cn and hold in back, k2, sl last st from cn back to LH needle and k1, k2 from cn

Gauge

17 sts and 21 rows = 4 inches/10cm in pat st
34 st panel = 8 inches
To save time, take time to check gauge.

Pattern Notes

Circular needle is used to accommodate large number of stitches. Do not join; work in rows. After slipping border sts to holder, keep first and last st in St st for selvage edge.

Afghan

With smaller needles, cast on 160 sts.
Work in garter st for 11 rows, inc 9 sts evenly across last WS row. (169 sts)
Change to larger needle.
Set up pat
Next row (RS): K 7 sts and place on holder, p1, referring to chart [work from A–C] 4 times, then from A–B once, p1, place rem 7 sts on 2nd holder.
Keeping first and last st in St st, work even in established pat for 9 reps, ending last rep with Row 25.
Do not cut yarn, leave work on needle.

Side Borders

Sl sts from first holder to smaller needle.
Join yarn and work in garter stitch until border, when slightly stretched, is same length as afghan, ending with a WS row.
Sl sts to main needle.
With RS facing, sew border to edge of afghan. When near top, adjust length of border if necessary.
Rep for second border.

Top Border

Beg with a RS row and smaller needle, k across 7 border sts, k 155 sts dec 9 sts evenly, k 7 border sts. (160 sts)
Work in garter st for 10 more rows.
Bind off knitwise on WS. ◆

Openwork Lattice

Design by Katharine Hunt

A classic blockwork pattern will add a timeless look to any room.

Skill Level
Intermediate***

Size
Approximately 51 x 58 inches, lightly blocked

Materials
- Brown Sheep Nature Spun, 100 percent wool worsted weight yarn (245 yds/100g per skein): 16 skeins meadow green #N56
- Size 10½ (6mm) 29-inch circular needle or size needed to obtain gauge
- Stitch holder

Gauge
14 sts and 21 rows = 4 inches/10cm in Openwork pat
To save time, take time to check gauge

Pattern Stitches
A. Border Pattern
Cast on 6 sts. Knit 1 row.
Row 1 (WS): K2, *yo, k2tog, yo, k2; rep from * across row. (7 sts)
Rows 2, 4, 6 and 8: Knit.
Row 3: K3, *yo, k2tog, yo, k2; rep from * across row. (8 sts)
Row 5: K4, *yo, k2tog, yo, k2; rep from * across row. (9 sts)
Row 7: K5, *yo, k2tog, yo, k2; rep from * across row. (10 sts)
Row 9: K6, *yo, k2tog, yo, k2; rep from * across row. (11 sts)
Row 10: Bind off 5 sts, k to end of row. (6 sts)
Rep Rows 1–10 for desired length.

B. Border Corner
Row 1 (WS): K2, yo, k2tog, yo, k2. (7 sts)
Row 2: K7.
Row 3: K3, yo, k2tog, yo, k2. (8 sts)
Row 4: K5, turn.
Row 5: K5.
Row 6: K8.
Row 7: K4, yo, k2tog, yo, k2. (9 sts)
Row 8: K4, turn.
Row 9: K4.
Row 10: K9.
Row 11: K5, yo, k2tog, yo, k2. (10 sts)
Row 12: K5, turn.
Row 13: K5.
Row 14: K10.
Row 15: K6, yo, k2tog, yo, k2. (11 sts)
Row 16: Bind off 5 sts, k to end. (6 sts)

Pattern Notes
Afghan is worked using 2 strands held tog throughout.
Circular needle is used to accommodate large number of sts. Do not join, work in rows.

Afghan
With 2 strands of yarn held tog, cast on 163 sts.
Knit 2 rows.
Referring to chart, work even until afghan measures approximately 53 inches, ending with row 24 of pat.
Knit 2 rows.
Bind off knitwise.

Finishing

Block afghan.

Work Border pat until length, when slightly stretched, is 1½ inches shorter than cast-on edge.

Work Border Corner.

Continue in Border pat until length measures about ⅔ of length of side edge. Sl sts to holder.

With RS tog, sew border along cast-on edge, starting ¾ inch from bottom left corner, easing corner to fit and then sewing border to side edge.

Sl border sts back to needle, continue working border and corner shapings, sewing as you go and adjusting length to fit if necessary.

After completing Row 16 of final corner, knit 1 row, then bind off knitwise.

Sew ends of border tog with a flat seam. ◆

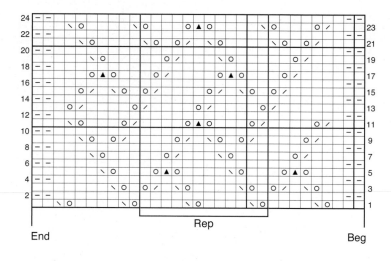

OPENWORK LATTICE CHART

STITCH KEY
☐ K on RS, p on WS
— P on RS, k on WS
⊙ Yo
╱ K2tog
╲ Ssk
▲ K3tog

Navajo Trail

Design by Diane Zangl

The woven Navajo Chiefs' blankets of the Southwest inspired this throw.

Skill Level
Intermediate***

Size
Approximately 40 x 46 inches

Materials
- Brown Sheep Lamb's Pride Bulky, 85 percent wool/15 percent mohair bulky weight yarn (125 yds/4 oz per skein): 6 skeins Aztec turquoise #M78, 4 skeins créme #M10, 3 skeins rust #M97
- Size 13 (9mm) 36-inch circular needle or size needed to obtain gauge
- Size K/10½ (6.5mm) crochet hook
- Tapestry needle

Gauge
9 sts and 12 rows = 4 inches/10cm in pat with 2 strands held tog
To save time, take time to check gauge.

Pattern Notes
Throw is worked in one piece using St st and stranded motifs. Two rounds of single crochet finish the edges.

Yarn is used doubled throughout.

Circular needle is used to accommodate large number of sts. Do not join; work back and forth in rows. Color pats are worked from charts, beg on a RS row the first time, on a WS row the next time.

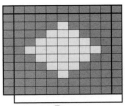

Rep

CHART A
DIAMONDS

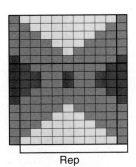

Rep

CHART B
MOUNTAINS

COLOR KEY
▨ Aztec turquoise
☐ Créme
▉ Rust

Throw

With 2 strands of turquoise held tog, cast on 91 sts.
Work in St st in following color sequence:
5 rows turquoise
2 rows rust
6 rows créme
2 rows rust
11 rows of Chart A—Diamonds
2 rows rust
4 rows créme
2 rows rust
6 rows turquoise
2 rows rust
16 rows of Chart B—Mountains
1 row turquoise
1 row créme
5 rows turquoise
2 rows rust (68 rows)

Rows 69–136: Work rows of color sequence in reverse order.
Bind off all sts.

Edging

With créme, work 1 rnd sc around entire throw, making sure to keep work flat. Join with sl st.

Rnd 2: With rust, work 1 sc in each sc of previous rnd, working 2 sc in each corner st. Join with sl st. Fasten off. ◆

Gray Rose

Design by Dixie Butler

A combination of two colors gives a heathery look
to a first-project afghan.

Skill Level
Beginner*

Size
Approximately 46 x 60 inches, without fringe

Materials
- Brown Sheep Nature Spun, 100 percent wool worsted weight yarn (245 yds/100g per skein): 10 skeins grey heather #N03 (MC), 5 skeins cranberry fog #N81 (CC)
- Size 17 (12mm) needles or size needed to obtain gauge

Gauge
9 sts and 13 rows = 4 inches/10cm in pat st
To save time, take time to check gauge.

Pattern Notes
Afghan is worked with 2 strands of MC and 1 strand of CC held tog throughout.
Sl all sts purlwise.

Afghan
Cast on 100 sts.
Rows 1 (RS) and 2: Sl 1, k1, *p1, k1; rep from * across row.
Rows 3 and 7: Sl 1, k to end of row.
Row 4: Sl 1, p to last st, k1.
Rows 5 and 6: Sl 1, *p1, k1; rep from * across row.
Row 8: Rep Row 4.
Rep Rows 1–8 until afghan measures approximately 60 inches, ending with Row 2 or 6 of pat.
Bind off.

Fringe
Cut strands of yarn, each 12 inches long.
For each fringe, use 2 strands CC and 4 strands MC held tog.
Fold group in half and knot into each st of bound-off edge.
Rep along cast-on edge. ◆

Diamond Lace

Design by Nazanin S. Fard

A diamond lace pattern worked on a garter stitch background makes a cozy afghan that is completely reversible. It is edged with reverse crochet stitch.

Skill Level
Easy**

Size
Approximately 50 x 60 inches

Materials
- Brown Sheep Lamb's Pride Superwash Bulky, 100 percent washable wool bulky weight yarn (110 yds/100g per skein): 15 skeins plum crazy #SW55
- Size 10½ (6.5mm) needles or size needed to obtain gauge
- Size J/10 crochet hook

Gauge
12 sts and 24 rows (12 ridges) = 4 inches/10cm in garter st
To save time, take time to check gauge

Pattern Stitch
Diamond Lace
(Multiple of 18 sts + 5)
Row 1–6: Knit.
Row 7: *K2tog, yo; rep from * across, end last rep k1.
Row 8–12: Knit.
Row 13: K10, *k2tog, yo, k16; rep from * across, end last rep k11.
Row 14 and all even-numbered rows: Knit.
Row 15: K9, *k2tog, yo, k1, yo, ssk, k13; rep from * across, end last rep k9.
Row 17: K8, *k2tog, yo, k3, yo, ssk, k11; rep from * across, end last rep k8.
Row 19: K7, *k2tog, yo, k5, yo, ssk, k9; rep from * across, end last rep k7.

Row 21: K6, *k2tog, yo, k7, yo, ssk, k7; rep from * across, end last rep k6.
Row 23: K5, *k2tog, yo, k9, yo, ssk, k5; rep from * across row.
Row 25: K4, *k2tog, yo, k11, yo, ssk, k3; rep from * across, end last rep k4.
Row 27: K6, *yo, ssk, k7, k2tog, yo, k7; rep from * across, end last rep k6.
Row 29: K7, *yo, ssk, k5, k2tog, yo, k9; rep from * across, end last rep k7.
Row 31: K8, *yo, ssk, k3, k2tog, yo, k11; rep from * across, end last rep k8.
Row 33: K9, *yo, ssk, k1, k2tog, yo, k13; rep from * across, end last rep k9.
Row 35: K10, *yo, sl 1, k2tog, psso, yo, k15; rep from * across, end last rep k10.
Row 37: K11, yo, ssk, k16; rep from * across, end last rep k10.
Row 39–42: Knit.
Rep Rows 1–42 for pat.

Afghan
Cast on 149 sts.
Work even in Diamond Lace pat until afghan measures 60 inches.
Bind off loosely, do not cut yarn.

Edging
Rnd 1: With crochet hook, sc in every st along cast-on and bound-off edges and every other row on side edges. Join with sl st, do not turn.
Rnd 2: Working from left to right, work 1 sc in each sc of previous rnd. Join with sl st, fasten off. ◆

Bavarian Beauty

Design by Lois S. Young

Traveling Bavarian twist stitches
make an elegant afghan to
treasure always.

Skill Level
Advanced****

Size
Approximately 41 x 64 inches

Materials
• Brown Sheep Nature Spun, 100 percent wool worsted weight yarn
  (245 yards/100g per skein): 13 skeins antique turquoise #N76
• Size 11 (8mm) needles or size needed to obtain gauge
• Stitch markers
• Cable needle

Gauge
14 sts and 15 rows = 4 inches/10cm in pat st
To save time, take time to check gauge.

Pattern Notes
Two strands of yarn are held tog for entire afghan.
Sl first st of each row knitwise.
Charts are written in Bavarian style. The diagonal line between chart rows
indicates the direction the stitch travels.
All foreground sts are worked through the back loop. Background sts are
Reverse St st.
For ease in working pats, pm between each panel.

Afghan
Cast on 131 sts.
Rows 1–8: Sl 1, k to end of row.
Set up pat
Next row (RS): Sl 1, k4, p2, work Row 1 of Chart A, p3, Chart B, p3, Chart
A, p3, Chart C, p3, Chart D, p3, Chart B, p3, Chart D, p2, k5.
Keeping 5 sts at each end in garter st and sts between panels in Reverse St st,

work even in established chart pats until 15 reps of
Chart B have been completed.

Work even for 15 more rows.

Next 9 rows: Sl 1, k to end of row.

Bind off knitwise on WS. ◆

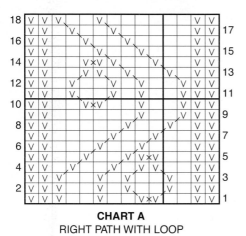

CHART A
RIGHT PATH WITH LOOP

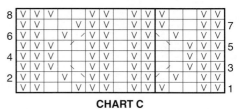

CHART C
MOUNTAIN PATHS

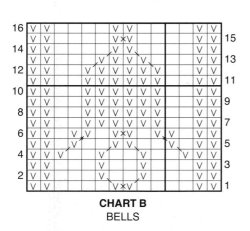

CHART B
BELLS

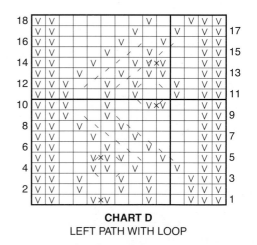

CHART D
LEFT PATH WITH LOOP

Tile Paths

Design by Diane Zangl

Inspiration comes from many sources—this design evolved from a tile floor. It is the perfect size to cover your lap on a chilly evening.

Skill Level
Intermediate***

Finished Size
Approximately 40 x 45 inches (throw); 49 x 54 inches (afghan)
Instructions are given for throw, with afghan in parentheses. When only 1 number is given, it applies to both sizes.

Materials
- Brown Sheep Nature Spun, 100 percent wool worsted weight yarn (245 yds/100g per skein): 4 (6) skeins pepper #601, 3 (5) skeins silver sage #107, 2 (3) skeins each natural #730, deep sea #103, beet red #235
- Size 10½ (6.5mm) straight and 29-inch circular needles or size needed to obtain gauge
- Tapestry needle

Gauge
13 sts and 17 rows = 4 inches/10cm in St st (blocked)
To save time, take time to check gauge.

Special Abbreviations
M1L (Make 1 Left): Make a clockwise backwards loop and place on RH needle.
M1R (Make 1 Right): Make a counter clockwise loop and place on RH needle. On next row, k in back of this st to avoid a hole.

Pattern Notes
Each individual block (or diamond actually) starts by casting on 3 sts and increasing outward in St st until the desired width is achieved. Then dec are worked until piece is back to its original starting size.
Yarn is used doubled throughout.
For the vertical stripe on Rows 21–33, cut a 2-foot length of yarn and fold it around the working color.
To avoid holes when changing colors, always bring new color up over old.
The pepper may be carried up the sides of the natural, deep sea and beet red sections to eliminate additional ends.

Block
Make 20 (30)
With black, cast on 3 sts.
Row 1 (WS): Purl.
Rows 2–4: Working in St st and referring to chart for color placement, [inc 1 st at each end every row] 3 times.
Row 5: Purl.
Rows 6–25: Rep Rows 2–5 until there are 39 sts.
Row 26: Rep Row 2 once.
Rows 27 and 28: Work 2 rows even.
Row 29: Dec 1 st each end of row.
Row 30: Knit.
Rows 31–33: [Dec 1 st at each end every row] 3 times.
Rows 34–51: Rep Rows 30–33, ending with Row 31. (7 sts remain)

Row 52: K2, sl 1, k2tog, psso, k2.
Row 53: P1, p3tog, p1.
Bind off 3 sts.

Finishing

Matching color stripes, sew squares tog to form a throw (afghan) 4 (5) squares wide and 5 (6) squares high.

Borders

With long circular needle and 2 strands of pepper, pick up and k 26 sts in each square along 1 edge of throw (afghan).
Knit 9 rows, inc 1 st at each end every other row.
Bind off all sts.
Rep for remaining 3 sides.
Sew corner seams. ◆

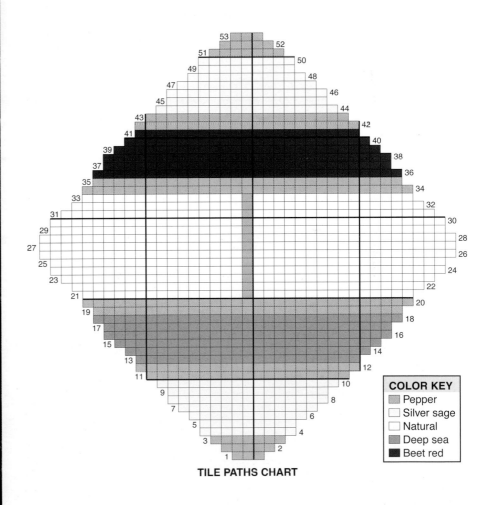

TILE PATHS CHART

COLOR KEY
- Pepper
- Silver sage
- Natural
- Deep sea
- Beet red

A Winter's Day

Design by Susan Robicheau

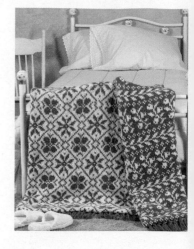

Two different designs create this lovely reversible bed quilt. A double layer makes it especially warm.

Skill Level
Intermediate***

Size
Approximately 48 x 52 inches, without fringe

Materials
• Brown Sheep Nature Spun, 100 percent wool worsted weight yarn (245 yds/100g per skein): 14 skeins each winter blue #117 and snow #740
• Size 11 (8mm) circular needle or size needed to obtain gauge
• Tapestry needle

Gauge
14 sts and 13 rows = 4 inches/10cm in color pat with 2 strands of yarn held tog
To save time, take time to check gauge.

Pattern Note
Afghan is worked with 2 strands held tog throughout.

Afghan

Front
With 2 strands of blue held tog, cast on 170 sts.
Row 1 (RS): Knit.
Row 2: K1, p to last st, k1.
Keeping first and last st in blue garter st, [rep Rows 1–33 of Chart A] 5 times.
Rep Rows 1–3.
Work 2 more rows with blue only.
Bind off.

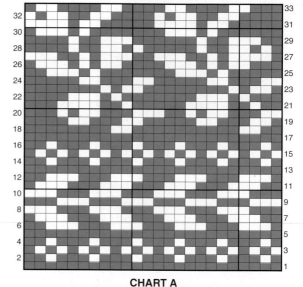

CHART A
FRONT

COLOR KEY
■ Winter blue
□ Snow

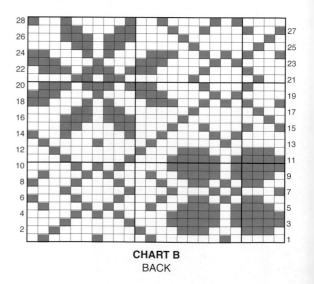

CHART B
BACK

Back

With 2 strands of white held tog, cast on 170 sts.
Row 1 (RS): Knit.
Row 2: K1, p to last st, k1.
Keeping first and last st in white garter st, [work Rows 1–28 of Chart B] 6 times.
Work 2 more rows with white only.
Bind off.

Finishing

Sew front and back tog on all sides.

Fringe

Cut strands of yarn, each 16 inches long.
Holding 4 strands tog, fold group in half.
Knot 1 group in every 4th st across cast-on edge.
Rep along bound-off edge. ◆

Reverse side of Winter's Day afghan

Summer Meadow
Continued from page 50

[Rep rows 2 and 3] twice.
Bind off.
Rep for other side of afghan.

Top Border

With B, pick up and k 125 sts along top of afghan, including side borders.
Work in pat, as for sides.
Rep for bottom of afghan, do not cut yarn.
Place last st on crochet hook.
Edging rnd: *Work 1 sc in each of next 2 sts, skip next st; rep from * around entire border, working 3 sc in each corner.
Join with sl st. Fasten off. ◆

Dotted Stripes
Continued from page 58

Rep Rows 1–18.
Work in Seed St for 6 rows.
Bind off in pat.

Side Borders
With MC and RS facing, pick up and k 148 sts
along one side edge.
Work in Seed St for 6 rows.
Bind off in pat. ◆

Sporty Squares
Continued from page 62

Afghan

Outside Panel
Make 2
With MC, cast on 21 sts.
[Work 1 Solid Square with MC, work 1 Bicolor
Square] 3 times, work 1 Solid Square with MC.

Panels 2 and 4
Make both alike
With CC, cast on 21 sts.
Work 1 Bicolor Square, [work 1 Solid Square with
MC, work 1 Solid Square with CC] twice, work 1
Solid Square with MC, work 1 Bicolor Square.

Center Panel
Make 1
With MC, cast on 21 sts.
[Work 1 Solid Square with MC, work 2 Solid
Squares with CC] 3 times, work 1 Solid
Square in MC.

Finishing
Block each panel.
Sew panels tog in order indicated.
Reblock lightly if necessary. ◆

FLOWER GARDEN

Diamond Lattice

Design by Lois S. Young

Pastel daisies bloom on a trellislike lattice. If care is taken with the embroidery, the afghan is truly reversible.

Skill Level
Beginner*

Size
Approximately 42 x 63 inches

Materials
- Brown Sheep Lamb's Pride Superwash Bulky, 100 percent washable wool bulky weight yarn (110 yds/100g per skein): 14 skeins white frost #SW11, small amounts strawberry chiffon #SW135, misty blue #SW71 and corn silk #SW13
- Size 10½ (6.5mm) needles or size needed to obtain gauge
- Tapestry needle

Gauge
12 sts and 14 rows = 4 inches/10cm in St st
To save time, take time to check gauge.

Pattern Notes
Two strands of yarn are held tog for entire afghan.
A single strand is used for embroidery.
Sl the first st of each row purlwise.
Keep 4 sts at each side of afghan in garter st for border.

Afghan
Cast on 141 sts.
Beg with a WS row, knit 7 rows, slipping first st of each row.
Set up pat
Next row (RS): Sl 1, k3, [work Row 1 of Chart A] 7 times, k4.
Continue to work even in established pats, rep 36 rows of [Chart A] twice, [Chart B] twice, [Chart A] once, [Chart B] twice, and finally [Chart A] twice.

Rep Row 1 of Chart A.
Knit 6 rows, slipping first st of each row.
Bind off knitwise on WS.

Embroidery
Referring to small photo below for placement and
colorway, embroider a 6-petal flower in center of
plain diamond using lazy daisy st.
With C, embroider four French knots in
center of each daisy. ◆

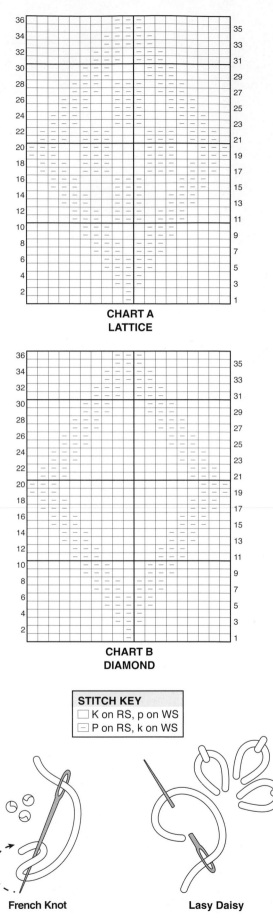

CHART A
LATTICE

CHART B
DIAMOND

STITCH KEY
☐ K on RS, p on WS
⊟ P on RS, k on WS

French Knot   **Lasy Daisy**

Bunches of Violets

Design by Lois S. Young

Bouquets of spring violets bloom in a carefully gridded garden.

Skill Level
Intermediate***

Size
Approximately 43 x 53 inches

Materials
- Brown Sheep Lamb's Pride Superwash Worsted, 100 percent washable wool worsted weight yarn (200 yds/100g per skein): 12 skeins prairie sage #SW160 (MC), 4 skeins mysterious fuchsia #SW27 (A), 1 skein plum crazy #SW55 (B)
- Size 7 (4.5mm) 16-inch circular or 2 double-pointed needles
- Size 11 (7mm) needles or size needed to obtain gauge
- Tapestry needle

Gauge
11 sts and 13 rows = 4 inches in St st with larger needles
To save time, take time to check gauge.

Pattern Stitch
Blocks
Odd-numbered rows 1–9 and 21–29 (RS): K1, [p1, k1] twice, *p7, k7, p7, k21, rep from * across, end last rep p7, k7, p7, k22, [p1, k1] twice.
All even-numbered rows: K1, [p1, k1] twice, k the knit sts and p the purl sts to last 5 sts, k1, [p1, k1] twice.
Odd-numbered rows 11–19: K1, [p1, k1] twice, *k7, p7, k7, k21, rep from * across, end last rep k7, p7, k7, k22, [p1, k1] twice.

Odd-numbered rows 31–39 and 51–59: K1, [p1, k1] twice, *k21, p7, k7, p7, rep from * across, end last rep k21, p7, k7, p7, k1, [p1, k1] twice.
Odd-numbered rows 41–49: K1, [p1, k1] twice, *k21, k7, p7, k7, rep from * across, end last rep k21, k1 [p1, k1] twice.

Pattern Notes
Two strands of MC are held tog for entire afghan. Violets are worked with a single strand.

Afghan
With larger needles and MC, loosely cast on 115 sts.
Next 8 rows: *K1, p1, rep from * across, end last rep k1.
[Work Rows 1–60 of Blocks pat] 3 times, rep Rows 1–30.
Next 8 rows: *K1, p1, rep from * across, end last rep k1.
Bind off purlwise on RS of work.

Violets
Make 72
Center
With B and smaller dpn or circular needle, make a sl knot and place on RH needle.
*Cast on 3 sts by making backward loop onto RH needle, turn.
Bind off 3 sts. (1 st remains)

[Rep from *] 4 times. (5 center petals)
Join into circle by picking up a st from base of first petal, bind off this st.
Cut B.

Petals
With RS facing, attach A between 1 set of center petals by putting tip of RH needle under 2 strands of yarn, put sl knot on tip of needle, draw this st to RS of work.
Push st to other end of needle, k1.

Row 1 (RS): Cast on 1 st by backward-loop method, pass first st over 2nd, cast on 1 st by backward-loop method. (2 sts)
Row 2: K1, (k1, p1) in next st. (3 sts)
Rows 3, 5, 7, 8, 9, 10, 12, 14 and 16: Knit.
Row 4: K2, (k1, p1) in next st. (4 sts)
Row 6: K3, (k1, p1) in next st. (5 sts)
Row 11: Bind off 1 st, k3. (4 sts)
Row 13: Bind off 1 st, k2. (3 sts)
Row 15: Bind off 1 st, k1. (2 sts)
Row 17: Bind off 1 st, pick up 1 st between next 2 center petals, pass first st over 2nd, cast on 1 st by backward-loop method. (2 sts)
[Rep Rows 2–17] 4 times.
On last rep, cut yarn and pull through last st after attaching between first set of center petals. Weave in ends, steam block each flower.

Finishing
With MC, sew one violet to center of each small knit square, referring to photo for placement. Hide ends between afghan and violet. ◆

Gingham Garden

Design by Barbara Venishnick

Flowers bloom on a gingham-check background.

Skill Level
Intermediate***

Size
Approximately 37 x 50 inches

Materials
- Brown Sheep Waverly Woolcolors, 100 per-cent wool bulky weight yarn (162 yds/4 oz per hank): 3 hanks each beige #1214 (A) and chocolate #1212 (C), 2 hanks natural #1005 (B), 1 hank each rose #2103 (D) and leaf green #5003 (E)
- Size 11 (8mm) 29-inch circular and 2 double-pointed needles or size needed to obtain gauge
- Tapestry needle

Gauge
14 sts and 24 rows = 4 inches/10cm in Gingham Checks pat
To save time, take time to check gauge.

Special Abbreviation
Cdd (centered double decrease): Sl 2 tog knitwise, k1, p2sso. Center st will lie on top of other 2.

Pattern Stitch
Gingham Checks
Row 1 (WS): With A, purl.
Row 2: With B, k1, sl 1 wyib, *k2, sl 2 wyib; rep from * across, end last rep sl 1 wyib, k1.
Row 3: With B, p1, sl 1 wyif, *p2, sl 2 wyif; rep from * across, end last rep p2, sl 1 wyif, p1.
Row 4: With A, knit.
Row 5: With C, p2, *sl 2 wyif, p2; rep from * across.

Row 6: With C, k2, *sl 2 wyib, k2; rep from * across.
Rep Rows 1–6 for pat.

Pattern Notes
Circular needles are used to accommodate large number of sts. Do not join; work in rows. Carry colors not in use up side of work.

Afghan
With A and circular needle, cast on 122 sts. Work even in Gingham Checks pat until afghan measures approximately 48 inches, ending with Row 1 of pat.
Bind off all sts.

Side Border
With C and circular needle, pick up and k 137 sts along left edge of afghan.
Knit 4 rows.
Bind off all sts knitwise on WS.
Rep border along right edge.

Lower Border
With C and circular needle, pick up and k122 sts along cast-on edge.
Turn, k122, turn.
Pick up and k 1 st at the beg of right side trim, k122, pick up and k 1 st at beg of left side trim.
Turn, k124, turn.
Pick up and k 1 st in next row of left side trim, k124, pick up and k1 st in next row of right side trim.

Turn, k126, turn.
Bind off all sts knitwise on WS.
Rep border along bound-off edge.

Appliqué

Flower Petals
Make 12
With D, cast on 5 sts
Row 1 (WS): P4, sl 1 wyif.
Row 2: K1-tbl, [k1, yo] twice, k1, sl 1 wyif.
Row 3: K1-tbl, p5, sl 1 wyif.
Row 4: K1-tbl, k2, yo, k1, yo, k2, k1-tbl.
Row 5: K1-tbl, p7, sl 1 wyif.
Row 6: K1-tbl, k3, yo, k1, yo, k3, sl 1 wyif.
Rows 7, 9 and 11: K1-tbl, p9, sl 1 wyif.
Rows 8 and 10: K1-tbl, k9, sl 1 wyif.
Row 12: Sl 2 wyib, pass first sl st over 2nd sl st, bind off 1 st, k5, k2tog, sl 1 wyib. (8 sts)
Row 13: Sl 2 wyif, pass first sl st over 2nd sl st, bind off 1 st purlwise, p2tog, sl 1 wyif. (5 sts)
Row 14: Sl 2 wyib, pass first sl st over 2nd sl st, k2tog, sl 1 wyib. (3 sts)
Row 15: Sl 2 wyif, pass first sl st over 2nd sl st, sl 1 wyif. (2 sts)
Row 16: Sl 2 sts wyib, pass first sl st over 2nd sl st, pull yarn through last loop.
Cut yarn, leaving a 12-inch end.

Leaf
Make 7
With E, cast on 3 sts.
Row 1 (WS): K1-tbl, p1, sl 1 wyif.
Row 2: K1-tbl, yo, k1, yo, sl 1 wyif. (5 sts)
Row 3: K1-tbl, p3, sl 1 wyif.
Row 4: K1-tbl, [k1, yo] twice, k1, sl 1 wyif. (7 sts)
Rows 5, 7, 9 and 11: K1-tbl, p5, sl 1 wyif.
Rows 6, 8 and 10: K1-tbl, k5, sl 1 wyif.
Row 12: K1-tbl, ssk, k1, k2tog, sl 1 wyif. (5 sts)
Row 13: K1-tbl, p3, sl 1 wyif.
Row 14: K1-tbl, cdd, sl 1 wyif. (3 sts)

Row 15: K1-tbl, p1, sl 1 wyif.
Row 16: Cdd, pull yarn through last loop.
Cut yarn, leaving a 12-inch end.

Flower Center
Make 3
With C and dpn, cast on 3 sts.
*Replace sts to LH needle, k3.
Rep from * until cord measures 8 inches. K3tog.
Cut yarn, leaving an 18-inch end.
Fasten off final st.

Finishing
Sew corner edges of border tog.
Roll I-cord in a spiral to form a flat disc. Using 18-inch end, sew coil tog, leaving enough end to sew disc to afghan.
Referring to Fig. 1, pin flowers and leaves to afghan.
Sew appliqués in place using ends attached to each piece. ◆

Fig. 1
Appliqué Placement

Flowers on the Fence

Design by Jean Schafer-Albers

Celebrate the first days of spring with tulips and daffodils in the vibrant hues of the season.

Skill Level
Intermediate***

Size
Approximately 38 x 62 inches

Materials
- Brown Sheep Nature Spun, 100 percent wool worsted weight yarn (245 yds/100g per skein): 4 skeins each arctic moss #N20, meadow green #N56, evergreen #N24 (A), 1 skein each natural #730 (B), bougainvillea #105 (C), husker red #N44 (D), impasse yellow #305 (E), lullaby #307 (F), orange you glad #N54 (G), Victorian pink #N87 (H), pink please #N98 (I)
- Size 11 (8mm) 32-inch circular needle or size needed to obtain gauge
- Tapestry needle

Gauge
15 sts and 20 rows = 4 inches/10cm in St st
To save time, take time to check gauge.

Pattern Stitch
Seed Stitch (even number of sts)
Row 1 (WS): * K1, p1, rep from * across.

Row 2: * P1, k1, rep from * across.
Rep Rows 1–2 for pat.

Pattern Notes
Two strands of yarn are held tog for entire afghan.
MC consists of 1 strand each arctic moss and meadow green held tog.
Circular needle is used to accommodate large number of sts. Do not join; work in rows.
Picket fencing motif, leaves and stems are knit using stranded method; flower heads are knit in intarsia using a separate ball or bobbin for each color.
To avoid holes when changing colors, always bring new color up over old.

Afghan

Lower Border
With 2 strands of A held tog, cast on 134 sts.
Work in Seed st for 7 rows, inc 1 st on last row.
Set up pat
Next row (RS): With A work 6 sts in Seed st, with

MC work Row 1 of chart across next 123 sts, with A work 6 sts in Seed st.

Continue to work even in established pats until 143 rows of chart have been completed.

Turn chart upside down and complete second half of afghan in same manner by reading chart rows in reverse order.

Dec 1 st on final row by p2tog.

Top Border

With A, knit 1 row.

Work in Seed st for 6 rows.

Bind off in pat. ◆

COLOR KEY
☐ Arctic moss & meadow green combined (MC)
▨ Evergreen (A)
☐ Natural (B)
▮ Bougainvillea (C)
▮ Husker red (D)
▨ Impasse yellow (E)
☐ Lullaby (F)
▨ Orange you glad (G)
☐ Victorian pink (H)
▨ Pink please (I)

FLOWERS ON THE FENCE
LEFT SIDE

FLOWERS ON THE FENCE
RIGHT SIDE

Blossoms & Cables

Design by Lois S. Young

Open cables and small blossoms alternate in narrow panels on an Aran style afghan.

Skill Level
Intermediate***

Size
Approximately 42 x 54 inches

Materials
- Brown Sheep Lamb's Pride Superwash Bulky, 100 percent washable wool bulky weight yarn (110 yds/100g per skein): 14 skeins alabaster #SW10
- Size 11 (8mm) needles or size needed to obtain gauge
- Cable needle

Gauge
14 sts and 16 rows = 4 inches/10cm in pat st
To save time, take time to check gauge.

Special Abbreviations
Cross cable: Pull 3rd st on LH needle over first 2 sts, k1, yo, k1.
Right cross: Sl 1 st to cn and hold in back of work, k1-tbl, p1 from cn.
Left cross: Sl 1 st to cn and hold in front of work, p1, k1-tbl from cn.
Bobble: (K1, [p1, k1] twice) all in one st, turn, p5, turn. Sl 3 sts tog to RH needle, k2tog, pull each of remaining 3 sts over k2tog, 1 st at a time. Bring yarn to front of work, sl bobble to LH needle, take yarn to back of work, return bobble to RH needle, pulling yarn tightly. Wrapping prevents bobble from popping to WS of afghan.

Pattern Notes
Sl first st of each row purlwise.
On final rep of Chart A (Row 217), do not cross cables.

Afghan
Loosely cast on 145 sts.
Knit 7 rows, sl first st of each row.
Set up pat
Next row: Sl 1, k4, [work row 1 of Chart A, work Row 1 of Chart B] 7 times, rep Row 1 of Chart A, k5.
Work even in established pats until Chart B has been worked 12 times. (216 rows)
Rep Rows 1 and 2.
Knit 7 rows, sl first st of each row.
Bind off knitwise on WS. ◆

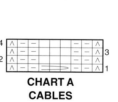

CHART A
CABLES

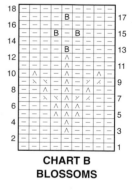

CHART B
BLOSSOMS

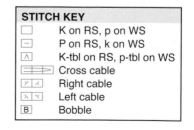

STITCH KEY

□	K on RS, p on WS
−	P on RS, k on WS
∧	K-tbl on RS, p-tbl on WS
⊟	Cross cable
⟋⟍	Right cable
⟍⟋	Left cable
B	Bobble

Tulip Time

Design by Susan Robicheau

Three different types of tulips bloom on an afghan worked in portable strips.

Skill Level
Advanced****

Size
Approximately 48 x 70 inches

Materials
- Brown Sheep Lamb's Pride Superwash Worsted, 100 percent washable wool worsted weight yarn (200 yds/100g per skein): 18 skeins blueberry sorbet #SW130
- Size 10½ (6.5mm) needles or size needed to obtain gauge
- Tapestry needle

Gauge
13 sts and 18 rows = 4 inches/10cm in St st with 2 strands of yarn held tog
To save time, take time to check gauge.

Pattern Stitches
Block A

Row 1 and all WS rows: K1, p to last st, k1.

Row 2: K7 [k2tog, yo] twice, k1 [yo, ssk] twice, k7.

Row 4: K6, k2tog, yo, k2tog, k1-tbl, yo, k1, yo, k1-tbl, ssk, yo, ssk, k6.

Row 6: K5, k2tog, yo, k2tog, k1, k1-tbl, yo, k1, yo, k1-tbl, k1, ssk, yo, ssk, k5.

Row 8: K4, k2tog, yo, k2tog, k2, k1-tbl, yo, k1, yo, k1-tbl, k2, ssk, yo, ssk, k4.

Row 10: K3, k2tog, yo, k2tog, k3, k1-tbl, yo, k1, yo, k1-tbl, k3, ssk, yo, ssk, k3.

Row 12: K2, k2tog, yo, k2tog, k4, k1-tbl, yo, k1, yo, k1-tbl, k4, ssk, yo, ssk, k2.

Row 14: K3, yo, ssk, k3, k2tog, yo, k1-tbl, k1, k1-tbl, yo, ssk, k3, k2tog, yo, k3.
Row 16: K3, yo, ssk, k2, [k2tog, yo] twice, k1, [yo, ssk] twice, k2, k2tog, yo, k3.
Row 18: K3, yo, ssk, k1, k2tog, yo, k2tog, k1-tbl, yo, k1, yo, k1-tbl, ssk, yo, ssk, k1, k2tog, yo, k3.
Row 20: K3, yo, ssk, k2tog, yo, k2tog, k1, k1-tbl, yo, k1, yo, k1-tbl, k1, ssk, yo, ssk, k2tog, yo, k3.
Row 22: K3, yo, sl 1, k2tog, psso, yo, k2tog, k2, k1-tbl, yo, k1, yo, k1-tbl, k2, ssk, yo, sl 1, k2tog, psso, yo, k3.
Row 24: K3, k1-tbl, k1, yo, ssk, k1, k2tog, yo, k1-tbl, k1, k1-tbl, yo, ssk, k1, k2tog, yo, k1, k1-tbl, k3.
Row 26: K5, yo, ssk, [k2tog, yo] twice, k1-tbl, [yo, ssk] twice, k2tog, yo, k5.
Row 28: K5, yo, sl 1, k2tog, psso, yo, k2tog, yo, k1-tbl, k1, k1-tbl, yo, ssk, yo, sl 1, k2tog, psso, yo, k5.
Row 30: K5, k1-tbl, k1, [yo, ssk] twice, k1, [k2tog, yo] twice, k1, k1-tbl, k5.
Row 32: K7, k1-tbl, yo, ssk, yo, sl 1, k2tog, psso, yo, k2tog, yo, k1-tbl, k7.
Row 34: K8, k1-tbl, yo, ssk, k1, k2tog, yo, k1-tbl, k8.
Row 36: K9, k1-tbl, yo, sl 1, k2tog, psso, yo, k1-tbl, k9.

Block B
Rows 1 and 3 (WS): Knit.
Rows 2 and 4: Purl.
Rows 5 and 7: K10, p3, k10.
Row 6: P10, k3, p10.
Row 8: P2, p2tog, p6, [k1, yo] twice, k1, p6, p2tog, p2.
Row 9: K9, p5, k9.
Row 10: P2, p2tog, p5, k2, yo, k1, yo, k2, p5, p2tog, p2.
Row 11: K8, p7, k8.
Row 12: P2, p2tog, p4, k3, yo, k1, yo, k3, p4, p2tog, p2.
Row 13: K7, p9, k7.
Row 14: P2, p2tog, p3, k4, yo, k1, yo, k4, p3, p2tog, p2.
Row 15: K6, p11, k6.
Row 16: P2, p2tog, p2, k5, yo, k1, yo, k5, p2, p2tog, p2.
Rows 17, 19, 21, 23 and 25: K5, p13, k5.
Row 18: P5, ssk, k4, yo, k1, yo, k4, k2tog, p5.
Row 20: P5, ssk, [k3, yo] twice, k3, k2tog, p5.
Row 22: P5, ssk, k2, yo, k2tog, yo, k1, yo, ssk, yo, k2, k2tog, p5.
Row 24: P5, ssk, k1, yo, k2tog, yo, k3, yo, ssk, yo, k1, k2tog, p5.
Row 26: P5, ssk, k1, yo, ssk, yo, k3, yo, k2tog, yo, k1, k2tog, p5.
Row 27: K7, p9, k7.
Row 28: P7, k1, yo, ssk, yo, sl 1, k2tog, psso, yo, k2tog, yo, k1, p7.
Row 29: K8, p7, k8.
Row 30: P8, k1, yo, ssk, k1, k2tog, yo, k1, p8.
Row 31: K9, p5, k9.
Row 32: P9, k1, yo, sl 1, k2tog, psso, yo, k1, p9.
Rows 33 and 35: Knit.
Rows 34 and 36: Purl.

Block C
Row 1 and all WS rows: K1, p to last st, k1.
Rows 2 and 4: Knit.
Row 6: K6, k2tog, yo, k1, yo, k2tog, k1, ssk, yo, k1, yo, ssk, k6.
Row 8: K5, k2tog, yo, k2, yo, k2tog, k1, ssk, yo, k2, yo, ssk, k5.
Row 10: K4, k2tog, yo, k3, yo, k2tog, k1, ssk, yo, k3, yo, ssk, k4.
Row 12: K3, k2tog, yo, k4, yo, k2tog, k1, ssk, yo, k4, yo, ssk, k3.
Row 14: K2, k2tog, yo, k5, yo, k2tog, k1, ssk, yo, k5, yo, ssk, k2.
Row 16: K3, yo, k2tog, k2, [k2tog, yo] twice, k1, [yo, ssk] twice, k2, ssk, yo, k3.
Row 18: K3, yo, k2tog, k1, [k2tog, yo] twice, k3, [yo, ssk] twice, k1, ssk, yo, k3.
Row 20: K3, yo, [k2tog] twice, yo, k2tog, yo, k5, yo, ssk, yo, [ssk] twice, yo, k3.
Row 22: K3, yo, sl 2, k1, p2sso, yo, k2tog, yo, k7, yo, ssk, yo, sl 2, k1, p2sso, yo, k3.
Row 24: K3, k2tog, yo, k2, yo, k2tog, k5, ssk, yo, k2, yo, ssk, k3.
Row 26: K7, yo, k2tog, k5, ssk, yo, k7.
Row 28: K7, yo, [k2tog] twice, yo, k1, yo, [ssk] twice, yo, k7.
Row 30: K7, yo, sl 2, k1, p2sso, yo, k3, yo, sl 2, k1, p2sso, yo, k7.
Rows 32, 34 and 36: Knit.

Pattern Notes
Two strands of yarn are held tog for entire afghan. Afghan is worked in strips; see chart for placement of blocks.

Incs on border are made by knitting into front and back of next st.

Afghan

Cast on 23 sts for each strip.

Referring to chart for placement, work 6 strips of 8 blocks each.

Bind off final block of each strip.

Sew strips tog, using a single strand of yarn.

Border

Cast on 5 sts.

Row 1 (RS): K2, yo, k1, yo, k2.

Row 2: P6, k into front and back of next st (inc made).

Row 3: K1, p1, k2, yo, k1, yo, k3.

Row 4: P8, inc, k1.

Row 5: K1, p2, k3, yo, k1, yo, k4.

Row 6: P10, inc, k2.

Row 7: K1, p3, k4, yo, k1, yo, k5.

Row 8: P12, inc, k3.

Row 9: K1, p4, ssk, k7, k2tog, k1.

Row 10: P10, inc, k4.

Row 11: K1, p5, ssk, k5, k2tog, k1.

Row 12: P8, inc, k2, p1, k2.

Row 13: K1, p1, k1, p4, ssk, k3, k2tog, k1.

Row 14: P6, inc, k3, p1, k2.

Row 15: K1, p1, k1, p5, ssk, k1, k2tog, k1.

Row 16: P4, inc, k4, p1, k2.

Row 17: K1, p1, k1, p6, sl 1, k2tog, psso, k1.

Row 18: P2tog, bind off next 5 sts using p2tog to bind off first st, p3, k1.

Rep Rows 1–18 for pat.

[Work Rows 1–18 of Border pat] 46 times or until border fits around entire afghan. Sl sts to holder and sew border to afghan, adjusting length as necessary when you near the end.

On final Row 18, p2tog, bind off rem sts.

Join border edges tog, and sew remaining area to afghan.

Block. ◆

A	B	A	B	A	C
C	A	B	A	B	A
A	B	C	B	C	B
B	A	B	A	B	A
A	B	C	B	C	B
B	A	B	A	B	A
A	B	A	B	A	C
C	A	B	A	B	A

ASSEMBLY CHART

Flora **Dora**

Design by Kathleen Power Johnson

This afghan is
worked in one piece
in bands of repeating
blossoms. Each band
is separated by
picot-accented
edging that is
applied after the
afghan is complete.

Skill Level
Easy**

Size
Approximately 48 x 60 inches, without edging

Materials
- Brown Sheep Lamb's Pride Worsted, 85 percent wool/15 percent mohair worsted weight yarn (190 yds/4 oz per skein): 13 skeins lotus pink #M38 (MC), 2 skeins white frost #M11 (A)
- Brown Sheep Lamb's Pride Bulky, 85 percent wool/15 percent mohair bulky weight yarn (125 yds/4 oz per skein): 1 skein white frost #M11 (B)
- Size 10 (6mm) 24-inch circular needle
- Size 11 (8mm) 36-inch circular needle or size needed to obtain gauge

Gauge
12 sts and 16 rows = 4 inches/10cm in St st with 2 strands of yarn on larger needles
To save time, take time to check gauge.

Special Abbreviation
Picot: Cast on 2 sts, bind off these two sts.

Pattern Stitch
Eyelet Blossoms
Row 1 (RS): K8, *[k2tog] twice, yo, (k1, p1, k1) into next st, yo, [ssk] twice, k10, rep from * across, end last rep k8.
Row 2 (and all even-numbered rows): Purl.
Row 3: K8, *[k2tog, yo] twice, k1, [yo, ssk] twice, k10, rep from * across, end last rep k8.
Row 5: K7, *k2tog, yo, k2tog, [k1, yo] twice, k1, ssk, yo, ssk, k8, rep from * across, end last rep k7.
Row 7: K6, *k2tog, yo, k2tog, k2, yo, k1, yo, k2, ssk, yo, ssk, k6, rep from * across.
Row 9: K6, *k2tog, yo, k1, k2tog, yo, k3, yo, ssk, k1, yo, ssk, k6, rep from * across.
Row 11: K6, *[k2tog, yo] twice, k5, [yo, ssk] twice, k6, rep from * across.
Row 13: K10, *yo, ssk, k1, k2tog, yo, k14, rep from * across, end last rep k10.
Row 15: K11, *yo, sl 1 knitwise, k2tog, psso, yo, k16, rep from * across, end last rep k11.
Row 16: Purl.

Pattern Notes
Two strands of yarn are held tog for entire afghan. Circular needles are used to accommodate large number of sts. Do not join; work in rows.

Afghan
With larger needles and MC, loosely cast on 139 sts.
*Work in St st for 6 rows, ending with a WS row.
Work 16 rows of Eyelet Blossoms pat, then 6 rows of St st.

With A, knit 2 rows.
Rep from * 6 times, ending last rep with 2nd 6 rows of St st.
Bind off loosely.

Picot Bands
Work in each garter-st stripe that separates bands.
Row 1: With smaller needles and 1 strand of B, beg with 2nd st pick up and k 1 st in each down-curving garter st 'bump' across row. Do not work last st. (137 sts)
Row 2: Bind off 4 sts, *slip last st back to LH needle, picot, bind off 3 sts, rep from * across, binding off last st.

Side Edging
With RS facing using larger needles and MC, pick up and k 179 sts along one long edge.
Knit 1 row.
Change to A and knit 1 more row.
Bind off.
Rep along remaining side edge.

Edging
With RS facing using larger needles and MC, pick up and k 144 sts across bound-off edge, including edge of trim.
Knit 1 row.
Change to A.
Next row: K1, *yo, k2tog, rep from * across, end last rep k1.
Purl 1 row.
Bind off purlwise.
Rep along cast-on edge. ◆

Nature's **First Green**

Design by JC Briar

Squares, knit from corner to corner, make great portable knitting projects. Sewn together, they form four-petaled flowers.

Skill Level
Intermediate***

Size
Approximately 40 x 60 inches

Materials
- Brown Sheep Lamb's Pride Bulky, 85 percent wool/15 percent mohair bulky weight yarn (125 yds/4 oz per skein): 12 skeins seafoam #M16
- Size 11 (8mm) needles or size needed to obtain gauge
- Tapestry needle
- Size H/8 crochet hook

Gauge
13 sts and 20 rows = 4 inches/10cm in St st
To save time, take time to check gauge.

Special Abbreviations
Cdd (centered double decrease): Sl 2 sts as if to k2tog, k1, pass 2 sl sts over.
Ssp (a decrease): Sl 2 sts knitwise 1 at a time to RH needle, place sts back on LH needle in this reversed position, p2tog.
M5 (Make 5 from 1): In next stitch, [k1, yo, k1, yo, k1].

Afghan Square
Make 24
Make a sl knot and place on LH needle, leaving a tail 36 inches long for later use in sewing squares tog.

Petal Section
Row 1 (RS): Yo, k1, k1-tbl. (3 sts)
Row 2: Yo, p3. (4 sts)
Row 3: Yo, p1, yo, k1, yo, p1, k1. (7 sts)
Row 4: Yo, k2, p3, k1, p1. (8 sts)
Row 5: Yo, p2, [k1, yo] twice, k1, p2, k1. (11 sts)
Row 6: Yo, k3, p5, k2, p1. (12 sts)
Row 7: Yo, p3, k2, yo, k1, yo, k2, p3, k1. (15 sts)
Row 8: Yo, k4, p7, k3, p1. (16 sts)
Row 9: Yo, p4, k3, yo, k1, yo, k3, p4, k1. (19 sts)
Row 10: Yo, k5, p9, k4, p1. (20 sts)
Row 11: Yo, p5, k4, yo, k1, yo, k4, p5, k1. (23 sts)
Row 12: Yo, k6, p11, k5, p1. (24 sts)
Row 13: Yo, p6, k5, yo, k1, yo, k5, p6, k1. (27 sts)
Row 14: Yo, k7, p13, k6, p1. (28 sts)
Row 15: Yo, p7, k6, yo, k1, yo, k6, p7, k1. (31 sts)
Row 16: Yo, k8, p15, k7, p1. (32 sts)
Row 17: Yo, p8, k2tog, k11, ssk, p8, k1. (31 sts)
Row 18: Yo, k9, p13, k8, p1. (32 sts)
Row 19: Yo, p9, k2tog, k9, ssk, p9, k1. (31 sts)
Row 20: Yo, k10, p11, k9, p1. (32 sts)
Row 21: Yo, p10, k2tog, k7, ssk, p10, k1. (31 sts)
Row 22: Yo, k11, p9, k10, p1. (32 sts)
Row 23: Yo, p11, k2tog, k5, ssk, p11, k1. (31 sts)
Row 24: Yo, k12, p7, k11, p1. (32 sts)
Row 25: Yo, p12, k2tog, k3, ssk, p12, k1. (31 sts)
Row 26: Yo, k13, p5, k12, p1. (32 sts)
Row 27: Yo, p13, k2tog, k1, ssk, p13, k1. (31 sts)
Row 28: Yo, k14, p3, k13, p1. (32 sts)
Row 29: Yo, p14, cdd, p14, k1. (31 sts)

Row 30: Yo, k30, p1. (32 sts)
Row 31: Yo, p31, k1. (33 sts)
Row 32: Yo, k32, p1. (34 sts)
Row 33: Yo, p33, k1. (35 sts)
Row 34: Yo, k34, p1. (36 sts)

Eyelet Section
Row 35: Yo, k2tog, k31, ssk, k1. (35 sts)
Row 36: Yo, ssp, p30, p2tog, p1. (34 sts)
Row 37: Yo, k2tog, k1, [yo, k2tog] 14 times, ssk, k1. (33 sts)
Row 38: Yo, ssp, p28, p2tog, p1. (32 sts)
Row 39: Yo, k2tog, k27, ssk, k1. (31 sts)

Bud Section
Row 40: Yo, ssp, k26, p2tog, p1. (30 sts)
Row 41: Yo, k2tog, p25, ssk, k1. (29 sts)
Row 42: Yo, ssp, k24, p2tog, p1. (28 sts)
Row 43: Yo, k2tog, [p5, M5] 3 times, p5, ssk, k1. (39 sts)
Row 44: Yo, ssp, [k5, p5] 3 times, k4, p2tog, p1. (38 sts)
Row 45: Yo, k2tog, p4, [k2tog, k1, ssk, p5] 2 times, k2tog, k1, ssk, p4, ssk, k1. (31 sts)
Row 46: Yo, ssp, k4, [p3, k5] twice, p3, k3, p2tog, p1. (30 sts)
Row 47: Yo, k2tog, p3, [cdd, p5] twice, cdd, p3, ssk, k1. (23 sts)
Row 48: Yo, ssp, k18, p2tog, p1. (22 sts)
Row 49: Yo, k2tog, [p5, M5] 2 times, p5, ssk, k1. (29 sts)
Row 50: Yo, ssp, [k5, p5] 2 times, k4, p2tog, p1. (28 sts)
Row 51: Yo, k2tog, p4, k2tog, k1, ssk, p5, k2tog, k1, ssk, p4, ssk, k1. (23 sts)
Row 52: Yo, ssp, k4, p3, k5, p3, k3, p2tog, p1. (22 sts)

Row 53: Yo, k2tog, p3, cdd, p5, cdd, p3, ssk, k1. (17 sts)
Row 54: Yo, ssp, k12, p2tog, p1. (16 sts)
Row 55: Yo, k2tog, p5, M5, p5, ssk, k1. (19 sts)
Row 56: Yo, ssp, k5, p5, k4, p2tog, p1. (18 sts)
Row 57: Yo, k2tog, p4, k2tog, k1, ssk, p4, ssk, k1. (15 sts)
Row 58: Yo, ssp, k4, p3, k3, p2tog, p1. (14 sts)
Row 59: Yo, k2tog, p3, cdd, p3, ssk, k1. (11 sts)
Row 60: Yo, ssp, k6, p2tog, p1. (10 sts)
Row 61: Yo, k2tog, p5, ssk, k1. (9 sts)
Row 62: Yo, ssp, [k2tog] twice, p2tog, p1. (6 sts)
Row 63: [K2tog] 3 times. (3 sts)
Row 64: P3tog.
Fasten off remaining st.
Cut yarn, leaving a tail 36 inches long for later use in sewing squares tog.

Finishing

Block each square to measure 11 x 11 inches.
Referring to photo and using 36-inch tails of yarn, sew 4 squares tog to form a larger square, having large petals at center. Join by sewing yo-edge loops of adjacent squares tog.
Sew resulting 6 squares tog to form afghan of 2 x 3 large squares.

Crochet Border

Join yarn in any yo-loop.
Work 2 sc in each yo-loop and 2 ch in each corner st.
Join with sl st and fasten off. ◆

Autumn **Blaze**

Design by Nazanin S. Fard

A colorful blaze of leaves
and berries is featured on
this lovely afghan. Worked
in panels, it is a handy
carry-along project.

Skill Level
Intermediate***

Size
Approximately 50 x 50 inches

Materials
- Brown Sheep Lamb's Pride Superwash Worsted, 100
  percent washable wool worsted weight yarn (200 yds/100g
  per skein): 18 skeins blaze #SW145
- Size 10 (6mm) needles or size needed to obtain gauge
- Tapestry needle

Gauge
14 sts and 22 rows = 4 inches/10cm in St st
To save time, take time to check gauge.

Special Abbreviations
M1 (Make 1): Lift the running thread between st just worked
and next st, k into the back of this thread.
P inc: P into front and back of next st.
K inc: K into front and back of next st.
Cdd (centered double decrease): Sl 2 tog knitwise, k1, p2sso.

Pattern Notes
Two strands of yarn are held tog for entire afghan.
Pay special attention to incs and decs, as st count varies in
both panels.

Afghan

Leaves Panel
Make 4
With 2 strands of yarn held tog, cast on 26 sts.
Rows 1 (WS)–4: Knit.
Row 5: K5, p5, k4, p3, k9.
Row 6: P7, p2tog, k inc, k2, p4, k2, yo, k1, yo, k2, p5.
Row 7: K5, p7, k4, p2, k1, p1, k8.
Row 8: P6, p2tog, k1, p inc, k2, p4, k3, yo, k1, yo, k3, p5.
Row 9: K5, p9, k4, p2, k2, p1, k7.
Row 10: P5, p2tog, k1, p inc, p1, k2, p4, ssk, k5, k2tog, p5.
Row 11: K5, p7, k4, p2, k3, p1, k6.
Row 12: P4, p2tog, k1, p inc, p2, k2, p4, ssk, k3, k2tog, p5.
Row 13: K5, p5, k4, p2, k4, p1, k5.
Row 14: P5, yo, k1, yo, p4, k2, p4, ssk, k1, k2tog, p5.
Row 15: K5, p3, k4, p2, k4, p3, k5.
Row 16: P5, [k1, yo] twice, k1, p4, k1, M1, k1, p2tog, p2, cdd, p5.
Row 17: K9, p3, k4, p5, k5.
Row 18: P5, k2, yo, k1, yo, k2, p4, k1, k inc, k1, p2tog, p7.
Row 19: K8, p1, k1, p2, k4, p7, k5.
Row 20: P5, k3, yo, k1, yo, k3, p4, k2, p inc, k1, p2tog, p6.
Row 21: K7, p1, k2, p2, k4, p9, k5.
Row 22: P5, ssk, k5, k2tog, p4, k2, p1, p inc, k1, p2tog, p5.
Row 23: K6, p1, k3, p2, k4, p7, k5.
Row 24: P5, ssk, k3, k2tog, p4, k2, p2, p inc, k1, p2tog, p4.
Row 25: K5, p1, k4, p2, k4, p5, k5.
Row 26: P5, ssk, k1, k2tog, p4, k2, p4, yo, k1, yo, p5.
Row 27: K5, p3, k4, p2, k4, p3, k5.
Row 28: P5, cdd, p2, p2tog, k1, M1, k1, p4, [k1,
yo] twice, k1, p5.
[Rep Rows 5–28] 10 times.
Knit 4 rows.
Bind off all sts loosely.

Berries Panel
Make 3
With 2 strands of yarn held tog, cast on 26 sts.
Rows 1 (WS)–4: Knit.
Row 5: *K2, p1; rep from * across, end last rep k2.
Row 6: *P2, [k1, p1] twice in next st, p2, k1; rep from * across, end last rep p2.
Rows 7 and 9: K2, *p1, k8; rep from * across.
Row 8: *P2, k4, p2, k1; rep from * across, end last rep p2.
Row 10: * P2, [k2tog] twice, pass first k2tog over 2nd, p2, k1; rep from * across, end last rep p2.
Row 11: Rep Row 5.
Row 12: *P2, k1, p2, [k1, p1] twice in the next st; rep from * across, end last rep p2.
Rows 13 and 15: *K8, p1; rep from * across, end last rep k2.
Row 14: *P2, k1, p2, k4; rep from * across, end last rep p2.
Row 16: *P2, k1, p2, [k2tog] twice, pass first k2tog over 2nd; rep from * across, end last rep p2.
[Rep rows 5–16] 20 times.
Knit 4 rows.
Bind off all sts loosely.

Finishing
Alternating Leaves and Berries panels, sew panels tog using single strand of yarn.

Side Border
With RS facing, pick up and k 130 sts evenly along one side edge.
Knit 3 rows.
Bind off loosely.
Rep for remaining side. ◆

English Garden

Design by Kathleen Power Johnson

Elementary panels are worked in Stockinette stitch and are later decorated with duplicate stitch and bobbles. The panels are joined and edged with crochet stitches.

Skill Level
Intermediate***

Size
Approximately 60 x 73 inches

Materials
- Brown Sheep Nature Spun, 100 percent wool worsted weight yarn (245 yds/100g per skein): 12 skeins enchanted forest #N25 (MC), 4 skeins Arctic moss #N20 (A), 3 skeins snow #740 (B), 2 skeins Victorian pink #N87 (C)
- Size 11 (8mm) needles or size needed to obtain gauge
- Size I/9 crochet hook

Gauge
12 sts and 20 rows = 4 inches/10cm in St st with 2 strands of yarn
To save time, take time to check gauge.

Pattern Notes
Two strands of yarn are held tog for entire afghan.
Sl first st of every row to form a chain stitch selvage.

Afghan

Lattice Panel
Make 2
With A, loosely cast on 21 sts.
Work even in St st until panel measures 73 inches.

Bind off loosely.
Referring to Chart A, duplicate st latticework onto panel.

Blossom Panel
Make 3
With MC, loosely cast on 45 sts.
Work in St st for 15 rows.
Referring to Chart B, mark the lower st of each leaf.
Work even in St st until panel measures 73 inches.
Bind off loosely.
Referring to Chart B and using markers to position first row, embroider leaves onto panel in duplicate st.
Make bobbles and attach to panel as indicated on Chart B.
Pull yarn ends to WS and tie tightly.

Bobble
With C, place a slip knot on LH needle, leaving a 3-inch tail.
Row 1: [K into front and back of st] twice, then k into front once more.
Work 3 rows St st.
Next row: Sl first 3 sts tog knitwise to the RH needle, k2tog, pass 2nd, then 3rd, then last st over first. Fasten off.

Finishing
With crochet hook and 2 strands of B, pull up a loop in lower corner of one panel, ch 1, pull up a loop in corresponding st on 2nd panel, *ch 1,

pull up a loop in st on opposite panel, moving up 1 row. Rep from * until panel is completely joined.
Rep for remaining panels.

Floret Edging

Rnd 1: Join B to edge of afghan near but not in corner st, ch 1. Work 1 rnd of sc around entire afghan, working 3 sc in each corner st and making sure to keep work flat. Join with sl st, turn.

Rnd 2: With C, ch 3,*sl st into next st, 1 dc in next st; rep from * around. Join with sl st at top of beginning ch-3. Fasten off. ◆

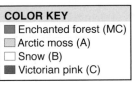

CHART A
LATTICE PANEL

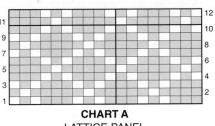

COLOR KEY
■ Enchanted forest (MC)
■ Arctic moss (A)
□ Snow (B)
■ Victorian pink (C)

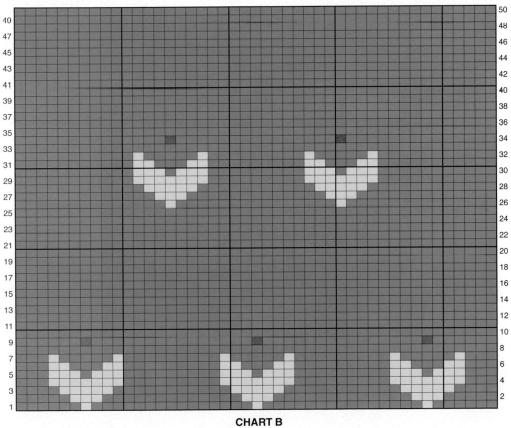

CHART B
BLOSSOMS

Hyacinth **Beauty**

Design by Frances Hughes

Puffy bud stitches combine with multiple yarn-overs to create a light and airy summer afghan.

Skill Level
Intermediate***

Size
Approximately 52 x 62 inches excluding fringe

Materials
- Brown Sheep Wildfoote Luxury Sock Yarn, 75 percent washable wool/25 percent nylon fingering weight yarn (215 yds/50g per skein): 20 skeins little lilac #SY32
- Size 11 (8mm) 32-inch circular needle or size needed to obtain gauge

Gauge
14 sts and 10 rows = 4 inches/10cm in pat st
To save time, take time to check gauge.

Pattern Stitch
Hyacinths
Row 1 (WS): K1, *p5tog, (k1, p1, k1, p1, k1) all in next st, rep from * across, end last rep k1.
Row 2: K1, purl to last st, k1.
Row 3: K1, *(k1, p1, k1, p1, k1) all in next st, p5tog, rep from * across, end last rep k1.
Row 4: K1, purl to last st, k1.
Row 5: Knit, wrapping yarn twice around needle for each st.
Row 6: K1, purl to last st dropping extra wrap for each st, k1.

Rep Rows 1–6 for pat.

Pattern Notes
Three strands of yarn are held tog for entire afghan. Circular needle is used to accommodate large number of sts. Do not join; work in rows.

Afghan
With 3 strands of yarn held tog, cast on 176 sts. Knit 2 rows.
Work even in Hyacinth pat until afghan measures 62 inches, ending with Row 3 of pat.
Next 2 rows: K1, purl to last st, k1.
Bind off loosely.

Double Knot Fringe
Cut strands of yarn, each 18 inches long.
Hold 5 strands tog and fold in half. Knot 1 group of strands in every 3rd cast-on st.
Divide strands, using 5 from left and 5 from right groups, and tie again about ¾ inch below first row of knots using an overhand knot.
Rep for another row of knots.
Rep fringe along bound-off edge. ◆

Climbing Vines

Design by Katharine Hunt

Vines and flowers frame
a central trellis. The outer
border is reminiscent of a
woven fence.

Skill Level
Advanced****

Size
Approximately 40 x 40 inches

Materials
- Brown Sheep Nature Spun, 100 percent wool worsted weight yarn (245 yds/100g per skein): 12 skeins Arctic moss #N20 (A), 1 skein snow #740 (B), small amount purple splendor #N60 (C)
- Size 9 (5.5mm) straight and circular needles
- Size 10 (6mm) straight and circular needles or size needed to obtain gauge
- Size 8 (5mm) needles for flowers
- Size E/4 crochet hook
- Cable needle
- Stitch markers
- Stitch holders
- Tapestry needle

Gauge
17 sts and 22 rows = 4 inches/10cm in Lattice Panel pat,
lightly blocked
To save time, take time to check gauge.

Special Abbreviations
C2R (Cross 2 Right): Sl next st to cn and hold in back, k1, k1 from cn.
C2L (Cross 2 Left): Sl next st to cn and hold in front, k1, k1 from cn.
T2B (Twist 2 Back): Sl next st to cn and hold in back, k1, p1 from cn.

T2f (twist 2 Front): Sl next st to cn and hold in front, p1, k1 from cn.

M1 (Make 1): Lift running strand between st just worked and next st, k into back of this strand.

Knit inc: Knit into front and back of next st.

Purl inc: Purl into front and back of next st.

Cdd (centered double decrease): Sl 2 sts knitwise, k1, pass 2 sl sts over. Center st will lie on top of other 2.

K1w2: K1 wrapping yarn twice around needle. Extra yarn will be dropped on following row.

Pattern Notes

Two strands of yarn are held tog for entire afghan. Flowers are worked with single strand.

Work selvage as a k st on every row on left edge of left panel and right edge of right panel. Selvage st is not included in instructions.

Pattern Stitches

A. Lattice Panel (multiple of 10 sts + 4)

Row 1 (WS): K6, p2, *k8, p2; rep from * to last 6 sts, k6.

Row 2: P5, t2b, t2f, *p6, t2b, t2f; rep from * to last 5 sts, p5.

Row 3: K5, p1, k2, p1, *k6, p1, k2, p1; rep from * to last 5 sts, k5.

Row 4: *P4, t2b, p2, t2f; rep from * to last 4 sts, p4.

Row 5: *K4, p1; rep from * to last 4 sts, k4.

Row 6: P3, t2b, p4, t2f, *p2, t2b, p4, t2f; rep from * to last 3 sts, p3.

Row 7: K3, p1, k6, p1, *k2, p1, k6, p1; rep from * to last 3 sts, k3.

Row 8: P2, *t2b, p6, t2f; rep from * to last 2 sts, p2.

Row 9: K2, p1, *k8, p2; rep from * to last 11 sts, k8, p1, k2.

Row 10: P2, k1,*p8, c2l; rep from * to last 11 sts, p8, k1, p2.

Row 11: K2, p1, *k8, p2; rep from * to last 11 sts, k8, p1, k2.

Row 12: P2, t2f, p6, t2b, *t2f, p6, t2b; rep from * to last 2 sts, p2.

Row 13: K3, *p1, k6, p1, k2; rep from * to last 11 sts, p1, k6, p1, k3.

Row 14: P3, *t2f, p4, t2b, p2; rep from * to last 11 sts, t2f, p4, t2b, p3.

Row 15: *K4, p1; rep from * to last 4 sts, k4.

Row 16: *P4, t2f, p2, t2b; rep from * to last 4 sts, p4.

Row 17: K5, *p1, k2, p1, k6; rep from * to last 9 sts, p1, k2, p1, k5.

Row 18: P5, *t2f, t2b, p6; rep from * to last 9 sts, t2f, t2b, p5.

Row 19: K6, *p2, k8; rep from * to last 8 sts, p2, k6.

Row 20: P6, *c2r, p8; rep from * to last 8 sts, c2r, p6.

Rep Rows 1–20 for pat.

B. Vine Leaf Panel

Section A (flower stem on right)

Row 1 (WS): K6, p5, k4, p3, k10.

Row 2: P8, p2tog, knit inc, k2, p4, k2, yo, k1, yo, k2, p6.

Row 3: K6, p7, k4, p2, k1, p1, k9.

Row 4: P7, p2tog, k1, purl inc, k2, p4, k3, yo, k1, yo, k3, p6.

Row 5: K6, p9, k4, p2, k2, p1, k8.

Row 6: P6, p2tog, k1, p1, purl inc, k2, p4, ssk, k5, k2tog, p6.

Row 7: K6, p7, k4, p2, k3, p1, k7.

Row 8: P5, p2tog, k1, p2, purl inc, k2, p4, ssk, k3, k2tog, p6.

Row 9: K6, p5, k4, p2, k4, p1, k6.

Row 10: P5, purl inc, k1, purl inc, p3, k2, p4, ssk, k1, k2tog, p6.

Row 11: K6, p3, k4, p2, k5, p1, k7.

Row 12: P6, purl inc, k1, purl inc, p4, k1, M1, k1, p2tog, p2, cdd, p6.

Row 13: K10, p3, k6, p1, k8.

Row 14: P8, k1, p6, k1, knit inc, k1, p2tog, p8.

Row 15: K9, p1, k1, p2, k6, p1, k8.

Row 16: P15, k2, purl inc, k1, p2tog, p7.

Row 17: K8, p1, k2, p2, k15.

Row 18: P15, k2, p1, purl inc, k1, p2tog, p6.

Row 19: K7, p1, k3, p2, k15.

Row 20: P13, p2tog, k2, p2, purl inc, k1, p2tog, p5.

Row 21: K6, p1, k4, p2, k14.

Row 22: [P5, p2tog] twice, k2, p3, purl inc, k1, purl inc, p5.

Row 23: K6, p3, k4, p2, k12.

Row 24: P5, p2tog, p3, p2tog, k1, M1, k1, p4, [k1, yo] twice, k1, p6.

Section B (two leaves)

Rows 1–10: Rep Rows 1–10 of Section A.

Row 11: K6, p3, k4, p2, k4, p3, k6.

Row 12: P6, [k1, yo] twice, k1, p4, k1, M1, k1, p2tog, p2, cdd, p6.

Row 13: K10, p3, k4, p5, k6.

Row 14: P6, k2, yo, k1, yo, k2, p4, k1, knit inc, k1, p2tog, p8.

Row 15: K9, p1, k1, p2, k4, p7, k6.

Row 16: P6, k3, yo, k1, yo, k3, p4, k2, purl inc, k1, p2tog, p7.

Row 17: K8, p1, k2, p2, k4, p9, k6.

Row 18: P6, ssk, k5, k2tog, p4, k2, p1, purl inc, k1, p2tog, p6.

Row 19: K7, p1, k3, p2, k4, p7, k6.

Row 20: P6, ssk, k3, k2tog, p4, k2, p2, purl inc, k1, p2tog, p5.

Row 21: K6, p1, k4, p2, k4, p5, k6.

Row 22: P6, ssk, k1, k2tog, p4, k2, p3, purl inc, k1, purl inc, p5.

Row 23: K7, p1, k5, p2, k4, p3, k6.

Row 24 (if the next section to be worked is Section A): P6, cdd, p2, p2tog, k1, M1, k1, p4, [k1, yo] twice, k1, p6.

Row 24 (if the next section to be worked is Section C): P6, cdd, p2, p2tog, k1, M1, k1, p4, purl inc, k1, purl inc, p6.

Section C (flower stem on left)

Row 1 (WS): K8, p1, k6, p3, k10.

Row 2: P8, p2tog, knit inc, k2, p6, k1, p8.

Row 3: K8, p1, k6, p2, k1, p1, k9.

Row 4: P7, p2tog, k1, purl inc, k2, p6, k1, p8.

Row 5: K8, p1, k6, p2, k2, p1, k8.

Row 6: P6, p2tog, k1, p1, purl inc, k2, p15.

Row 7: K15, p2, k3, p1, k7.

Row 8: P5, p2tog, k1, p2, purl inc, k2, p15.

Row 9: K15, p2, k4, p1, k6.

Row 10: P5, purl inc, k1, purl inc, p3, k2, [p2tog, p5] twice, p1.

Row 11: K13, p2, k4, p3, k6.

Row 12: P6, [k1, yo] twice, k1, p4, k1, M1, k1, [p2tog, p2] 3 times, p1.

Rows 13–24: Rep Rows 13–24 of Section B.

Afghan

Center Panel

With size 9 needles and 2 strands of A held tog, cast on 87 sts.
Knit 3 rows, inc 7 sts evenly on last RS row. (94 sts)
Change to larger needles.
[Work Rows 1–20 of Lattice Panel] 12 times.
Place sts on length of yarn.

Left Panel

With size 9 needles and 2 strands of A held tog, cast on 27 sts.
Knit 3 rows, inc 2 sts on last RS row as follows:
K17, M1, k3, M1, k6. (28 sts +1 selvage st)
Work sections in order of A, B, C, B, A, B, C, B, A, rep first 12 rows of Section B. Place sts on length of yarn.

Right Panel

Work as for left panel through inc row. (28 sts +1 selvage st)
Work sections in order of C, B, A, B, C, B, A, B, C, rep first 12 rows of Section B. Place sts on length of yarn.

Finishing

Block panels.
Referring to Fig. 1 on page 131, sew left panel with sts still on length of yarn to left edge of lattice panel, adjusting length as necessary to fit.
Sew right panel to right edge of lattice panel.
Place 29 stitches from right panel, 94 sts from lattice panel, and 29 sts from left panel onto size 9 circular needle. (152 sts)
Beg with a WS row, 3 rows, dec 11 sts evenly across first row. (141 sts)

Top Border

Row 1 (RS): With A, knit.

Row 2: P1, k to last st, p1.

Row 3: K1, M1, k to last st, M1, k1. (143 sts)

Row 4: Rep Row 2.

Row 5: Rep Row 3. (145 sts)

Row 6: Rep Row 2.

Row 7: Rep Row 3 (147) sts
Row 8: P1, k2, *k1w2, k3, rep from * to last 4 sts, k1w2, k2, p1. Change to B.
Row 9: K1, M1, k2, *sl 1, k3, rep from * to last 4 sts, sl 1, k2, M1, k1. (149 sts)
Row 10: P1, *k3, sl 1 wyif, rep from * to last 4 sts, k3, p1.
Row 11: K1, M1, k3, * sl 1, k3, rep from * to last st, M1, k1. (151 sts)
Row 12: P1, k4, sl 1 wyif, k3, rep from * to last 2 sts, k1, p1. Change to A.
Row 13: K1, M1, k to last st, M1, k1. (153 sts)
Row 14: P1, k to last st, p1.
Row 15: K1, M1, * knit to last st, M1, k1. (155 sts) Bind off.

Lower Border

With A and size 9 circular needle, pick up and k 141 sts along cast-on edge. Work as for top border, omitting decs of first row.

Side Borders

With A and size 9 circular needle, pick up and k 180 sts along side edge. Work as for top border, dec 7 sts evenly across first row. (173 sts)
Sew mitered corners of border.

Flower

Make 10
Beg at outer edge of petal with single strand of B and size 8 needle, cast on 3 sts.

Row 1 (RS): Knit.
Row 2 and all WS rows: Purl.
Row 3: K1, [M1, k1] twice. (5 sts)
Row 5: K1, M1, k3, M1, k1. (7 sts)
Row 7: K2, ssk, put this st on LH needle, pass 2nd st over first st, return st to RH needle, k2. (5 sts)
Row 8: Purl.
Cut yarn leaving a 10-inch tail. Slide petal to end of needle.
Make 4 more petals. Do not cut yarn after last petal. (25 sts)
Next Row (RS): Working across all petals and taking care not to spread sts apart, [k1, k2tog] 8 times, k1. (17 sts)
Row 2: [P1, p2tog] 5 times, p2tog. (11 sts)
Row 3: With C, p2, p2tog, p3, p2tog, p2. (9 sts)
Row 4: Knit firmly.
Cut yarn and draw through all sts twice.
Using yarn tails and crochet hook, work 10 sl sts around each petal edge.
With C, embroider a lazy daisy st on each petal as shown in photo on page 127.
Sew one flower to each stem on side panels. ◆

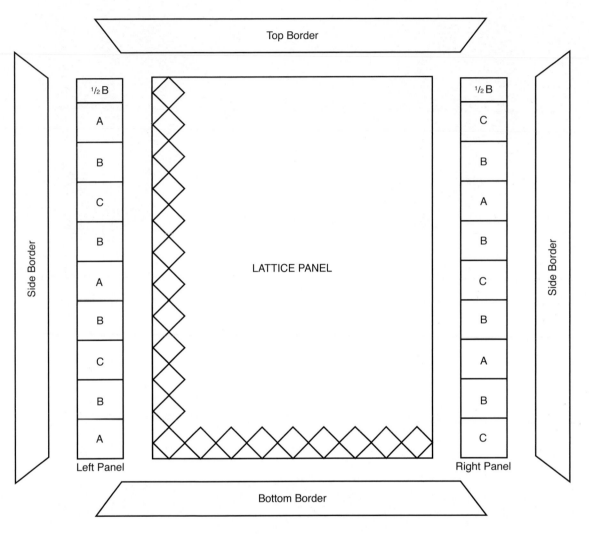

FIG. 1
ASSEMBLY

CLASSY **CABLES**

Romantic **Ruby**

Design by Melissa Leapman

Heart-shaped cables adorn a romantic red throw.
Make one for your sweetie for Valentine's Day.

Skill Level
Advanced****

Size
Approximately 45 x 54 inches, excluding fringe

Materials
- Brown Sheep Lamb's Pride Superwash Bulky, 100 percent washable wool bulky weight yarn (110 yds/100g per skein): 27 skeins romantic ruby #SW43
- Size 15 (10mm) 32-inch circular needle or size needed to obtain gauge
- Cable needle

Gauge
14 sts and 12 rows = 4 inches/10cm in cable pat
To save time, take time to check gauge.

Pattern Notes
Two strands of yarn are held tog for entire afghan.
Circular needle is used to accommodate large number of sts. Do not join; work in rows.

Afghan
With 2 strands of yarn held tog, cast on 152 sts.
Set up pat: Work Row 1 of Chart A over 20 sts, pm, beg and end as indicated, work Chart B over next 112 sts, pm, work Chart A over 20 sts.
Work even in established pats until afghan measures approximately 54 inches, ending with Row 2 of Chart B.
Bind off.

Fringe
Cut strands of yarn, each 16 inches long.
Holding 5 strands tog, fold each group in half.
Knot 1 group into every 3rd st along cast-on edge.
Rep along bound-off edge.
Trim fringe evenly. ◆

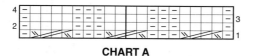

CHART A

STITCH KEY
☐ K on RS, p on WS
⊟ P on RS, k on WS
Sl 2 sts to cn and hold in front, k2, k2 from cn
Sl 2 sts to cn and hold in back, k2, k2 from cn
Sl 2 sts to cn and hold in front, p2, k2 from cn
Sl 2 sts to cn and hold in back, k2, p2 from cn
Sl next st to cn and hold in back, k2, p st from cn
Sl 2 sts to cn and hold in front, p1, k2 from cn

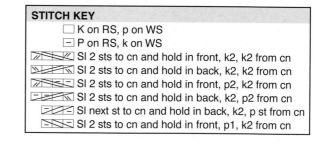

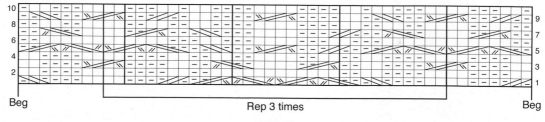

Beg   Rep 3 times   Beg

CHART B

Five **Easy Cables**

Design by Dixie Butler

Garter stitch and cable panels give a lot of bang for your buck in this easy afghan.

Skill Level
Easy**

Size
Approximately 44 x 52 inches

Materials
- Brown Sheep Prairie Silks, 72 percent wool/18 percent mohair/10 percent silk worsted weight yarn (88 yds/50g per skein): 32 skeins buck #PS450
- Size 13 (9mm) 29-inch circular needle or size needed to obtain gauge
- Cable needle

Gauge
11 sts and 16 rows = 4 inches/10cm in Garter & Cable pat.
To save time, take time to check gauge.

Special Abbreviations
Cf (cable front): Sl 3 sts to cn and hold in front, k3, k3 from cn.
Cb (cable back): Sl 3 sts to cn and hold in back, k3, k3 from cn.

Pattern Stitch
Garter & Cable
Rows 1 and 5 (RS): K10, *p2, k9; rep from * across, end last rep k10.
Row 2 and all WS rows: K9, p1, *k2, p9, k2, p1, k7, p1; rep from * across, end last rep p1, k9.
Row 3: K10, *p2, cf, k3, p2, k9; rep from * across, end last rep k10.
Row 7: K10, *p2, k3, cb, p2, k9; rep from * across, end last rep k10.
Row 8: Rep Row 2.
Rep Rows 1–8 for pat.

Pattern Notes
Two strands of yarn are held tog for entire afghan. Circular needle is used to accommodate large number of sts. Do not join; work in rows.

Afghan
With 2 strands of yarn held tog, cast on 121 sts. Work even in Garter & Cable pat until afghan measures approximately 52 inches, ending with Row 4 or 8 of pat.
Bind off in pat.
Block. ◆

Chocolate **Mousse**

Design by Kathy Cheifetz

A soft cotton and wool-blend yarn is used in a delicious, casual throw.

Skill Level
Easy**

Size
Approximately 45 x 60 inches

Materials
- Brown Sheep Cotton Fleece, 80 percent cotton/20 percent Merino wool light worsted weight yarn (215 yds/100g per skein): 18 skeins teddy bear #CW820
- Size 15 (10mm) 32-inch circular needle or size needed to obtain gauge
- Cable needle
- Size K/10 crochet hook

Gauge
11 sts and 14 rows = 4 inches/10cm in pat st
To save time, take time to check gauge.

Special Abbreviation
Mc (mini cable): Sl next stitch to cn and hold in front, k1, k1 from cn.

Pattern Stitch
Mini Cables
Rows 1, 3, 5, 7, 9 and 11 (RS): P4, *Mc, p4, rep from * across row.
Rows 2, 4, 6, 8, 10 and 12: K or p the sts as they present themselves.

Row 13: K4, *Mc, k4; rep from * across row.
Row 14: Purl.
Rows 15, 17, 19 and 21: Rep Row 1.
Rows 16, 18, 20 and 22: Rep Row 2.
Rows 23 and 24: Rep Rows 13 and 14.
Rep Rows 1–24 for pat.

Pattern Notes
Three strands of yarn are held tog for entire afghan. Circular needle is used to accommodate large number of sts. Do not join; work in rows.

Afghan
With 3 strands of yarn held tog, cast on 124 sts.
[Work Rows 1–24 of Mini Cables pat] 8 times, rep Rows 1–12.
Bind off in pat, do not cut yarn.

Edging
Place last st on crochet hook.
*Sl st loosely in every other st or row to corner st, ch 1, sc in corner st, ch 1, rep from * around entire afghan. ◆

Dimensional Triangles

Design by Joyce Englund

The triangles in this deeply textured throw are set off by subtle cables.

Skill Level
Intermediate***

Size
Approximately 47 x 63 inches

Materials
- Brown Sheep Lamb's Pride Worsted, 85 percent wool/15 percent mohair worsted weight yarn (190 yds/4 oz per skein): 24 skeins autumn harvest #M22
- Size 15 (10mm) 29-inch circular needle or size needed to obtain gauge
- Cable needle
- Stitch markers

Gauge
10½ sts and 15 rows = 4 inches/10cm in pat
To save time, take time to check gauge.

Special Abbreviations
C7f (cross 7 front): Slip 3 sts to cn and hold in front, k4, k3 from cn.
Cdd (center double decrease): Slip next 2 sts tog knitwise, k1, pass 2 sl sts over k st.

Pattern Stitches
A. Seed Stitch
Row 1 (RS): *K1, p1; rep from * across row.
Row 2: *P1, k1; rep from * across row.
Rep Rows 1–2 for pat.
B. Dimensional Triangles
Row 1 (RS): K6, yo, ssk, *k8, yo, ssk, rep from * to last 5 sts, k5.
Row 2 and all WS rows: Purl.

Row 3: K4, k2tog, yo, k1, yo, ssk, *k5, k tog, yo, k1, yo, ssk, rep from * to last 4 sts, k4.
Row 5: K3, *k2tog, yo, k3, yo, ssk, k3, rep from * across row.
Row 7: K2, *k2tog, yo, k5, yo, ssk, k1, rep from * to last st, k1.
Row 9: K1, k2tog, k7, *yo, CDD, yo, k7, rep from * to last 3 sts, yo, ssk, k1.
Row 11: K3, *c7f, k3, rep from * across row.
Row 12: Purl.
Rep Rows 1–12 for pat.

Pattern Notes
Three strands of yarn are held tog for entire afghan. Circular needle is used to accommodate large number of sts. Do not join; work in rows.

Afghan
With 3 strands of yarn held tog, cast on 125 sts.

Border
Knit 7 rows.
Set up pat: Seed st over 6 sts, pm, work Dimensional Triangles pat to last 6 sts, pm, Seed st over 6 sts.
Work even in established pats until afghan measures approximately 61 inches, ending with Row 9 of Dimensional Triangles pat.
Knit 7 rows.
Bind off knitwise. ◆

Ruble **Red**

Design by Joyce Englund

An openwork cable pattern enhances a luxurious silk-blend afghan.

Skill Level
Easy**

Size
Approximately 48 x 63 inches

Materials
• Brown Sheep Prairie Silks, 72 percent wool/18 percent mohair/10 percent silk worsted weight yarn (88 yds/50g per skein): 40 skeins ruble red #PS400
• Size 11 (8mm) 32-inch circular needle or size needed to obtain gauge
• Cable needle
• Stitch markers

Gauge
14 sts and 16 rows = 4 inches/10cm in Cable pat
To save time, take time to check gauge.

Special Abbreviations
Cdd (central double decrease): Sl next 2 sts tog knitwise, k1, p2sso.
C5f (cross 5 front): Slip next 2 sts to cn and hold at front of work, k3, k2 from cn.
Inc: K in each strand of next st.

Pattern Stitches
A. Seed Stitch
All rows: K1, *p1, k1, rep from * across row.
B. Cables
Row 1 and all WS rows: K3, *p5, k3, rep from * across row.
Row 2: P3, c5f, p3, *k1, yo, cdd, yo, k1, p3, c5f, p3, rep from * across row.

Row 4: P3, *k1, yo, cdd, yo, k1, p3, rep from * across row.
Row 6: P3, k1, yo, cdd, yo, k1, p3, *c5f, p3, k1, yo, cdd, yo, k1, p3, rep from across row.
Row 8: Rep Row 4.
Rep Rows 1–8 for pat.

Pattern Notes
Two strands of yarn are held tog for entire afghan.
Circular needle is used to accommodate large number of sts. Do not join; work in rows.

Afghan

Border
With 2 strands of yarn held tog, cast on 127 sts. Work even in Seed st pat for 7 rows.
Set up pat (RS): Seed st over 5 sts, pm, p3, *inc, k1, inc, p3, rep from * to last 5 sts, Seed st over 5 sts. (165 sts)
Keeping first and last 5 sts in Seed st and remaining sts in Cable pat, work even until afghan measures approximately 61 inches, ending with Row 3 of Cable pat.
Dec row (RS): Seed st over 5 sts, p3, * k1, cdd, k1, p3; rep from * to last 5 sts, Seed st over 5 sts. (127 sts)

Top Border
Work even in Seed st for 7 rows.
Bind off knitwise. ◆

Celtic **Tradition**

Design by Joyce Englund

Small cables and easy stitches form a block pattern in this traditional throw.

Skill Level
Easy**

Size
Approximately 48 x 63 inches

Materials
• Brown Sheep Lamb's Pride Superwash Worsted, 100 percent washable wool worsted weight yarn (200 yds/100g per skein): 17 skeins stonewashed denim #SW150
• Size 11 (8mm) 29-inch circular needle or size needed to obtain gauge
• Cable needle
• Stitch markers

Gauge
15 sts and 20 rows = 4 inches/10cm in Cable pat
To save time, take time to check gauge.

Special Abbreviation
C4 (cross 4): Slip next st to cn and hold in front, k 3rd st on LH needle, k first and 2nd sts, k1 from cn.

Pattern Stitch
Cables
Rows 1, 3 and 5 (RS): Knit.

Rows 2 and 4: P3, k2, *p5, k2; rep from * across, end last rep p3.
Rows 6 and 8: [K2, sl 1] twice, *k3, sl 1, k2, sl 1; rep from * across, end last rep k2.
Row 7: P2, sl 1, k2, sl 1, *p3, sl 1, k2, sl 1; rep from * across, end last rep p2.
Row 9: K2, C4, *k3, c4; rep from * across, end last rep k2.
Row 10: Rep Row 2.
Rep Rows 1–10 for pat.

Pattern Notes
Two strands of yarn are held tog for entire afghan.
Circular needle is used to accommodate large number of sts. Do not join; work in rows.

Afghan
With 2 strands of yarn held tog, cast on 165 sts.

Border
Knit 7 rows.
Set up pat: K7, pm, work in pat to last 7 sts, pm, k7.
Keeping first and last 7 sts in garter st and remaining sts in Cable pat, work even until afghan measures approximately 61 inches, ending with Row 2 of pat.
Knit 7 rows.
Bind off knitwise. ◆

Linked **Chains**

Design by Frances Hughes

Hefty cables interspersed with smaller ones make a perfect choice for a young man's college dorm room.

Skill Level
Intermediate***

Size
Approximately 50 x 60 inches

Materials
- Brown Sheep Country Classic Bulky, 100 percent wool bulky weight yarn (125 yds/4 oz per skein): 14 skeins cattail brown #R40
- Size 17 (12mm) 32-inch circular needles
- Cable needle

Gauge
7 sts and 9½ rows = 4 inches/10cm in pat st with 2 strands of yarn
To save time, take time to check gauge.

Special Abbreviations
C3l (cable 3 left): Sl 1 st to cn and hold in front, k2, k1 from cn.
C6r (cable 6 right): Sl 3 sts to cn and hold in back, k1, p1, k1, then k3 from cn.
C6l (cable 6 left): Sl 3 sts to cn and hold in front, k3, then k1, p1, k1 from cn.

Pattern Stitch
Cables
Row 1 (RS): K3, p3, k3, [k1, p1] 3 times, k3, p3, *sl 1 purlwise, k2, p3, k3, [k1, p1] 3 times, k3, p3; rep from * to last 3 sts, k3.
Row 2: K6, p3, [p1, k1] 3 times, p3, k3, *p2, sl 1 purlwise, k3, p3, [p1, k1] 3 times, p3, k3; rep from * to last 3 sts, k3.

Row 3: K3, p3, k3, [k1, p1] 3 times, k3, p3, *c3l, p3, k3, [k1, p1] 3 times, k3, p3; rep from * to last 3 sts, k3.
Row 4: K6, p3, [p1, k1] 3 times, p3, k3, *p3, k3, p3, [p1, k1] 3 times, p3, k3; rep from * to last 3 sts, k3.
Row 5: K3, p3, c6r, c6l, p3, *slip 1 purlwise, k2, p3, c6r, c6l, p3; rep from * to last 3 sts, k3.
Row 6: K6, p1, k1, p7, k1, p1, k4, *p2, sl 1 purlwise, k3, p1, k1, p7, k1, p1, k4; rep from * to last 3 sts, k3.
Row 7: K3, p3, k1, p1, k7, p1, k1, p4, *c3l, p3, k1, p1, k7, p1, k1, p4; rep from * to last 3 sts, k3.
Row 8: K6, p1, k1, p7, k1, p1, k4, *p3, k3, p1, k1, p7, k1, p1, k4; rep from * to last 3 sts, k3.
Row 9: K3, p3, k1, p1, k7, p1, k1, p4, *sl 1 purlwise, k2, p3, k1, p1, k7, p1, k1, p4; rep from to last 3 sts, k3.
Rows 10–13: Rep Rows 6–9.
Row 14: Rep Row 6.
Row 15: K3, p3, c6l, c6r, p3, *c3l, p3, c6l, c6r, p3; rep from * to last 3 sts, k3.
Row 16: Rep Row 4.
Rows 17–28: [Rep Rows 1–4] 3 times.

Pattern Notes
Two strands of yarn are held tog for entire afghan. Circular needles are used to accommodate large number of sts. Do not join; work in rows.

Afghan
With 2 strands of yarn held tog, cast on 87 sts.
Knit 4 rows.
Work Rows 1–28 of Cable pat, [rep Rows 5–28] 4 times, work Rows 5–17.
Knit 4 rows.
Bind off loosely. ◆

Misty **Blue**

Design by Melissa Leapman

Cables, entwined in a
bold lattice pattern, will
showcase your finest
knitting skills.

Skill Level
Advanced****

Size
Approximately 42 x 64 inches,
excluding fringe

Materials
- Brown Sheep Lamb's Pride Superwash Bulky, 100 percent washable
  wool bulky weight yarn (110 yds/100g per skein): 30 skeins misty
  blue #SW71
- Size 15 (10mm) 32-inch circular needle or size needed to
  obtain gauge
- 2 cable needles

Gauge
14 sts and 15 rows = 4 inches/10cm in pat st
To save time, take time to check gauge.

Pattern Notes
Two strands of yarn are held tog for entire afghan.
Circular needle is used to accommodate large number of sts.
Do not join; work in rows.
Only RS rows are shown on charts; for WS rows, k or p the sts
as they present themselves.

Afghan
With 2 strands of yarn held tog, cast on 150 sts.
Set up pat (RS): Work Row 1 of Chart A over 25 sts, pm, beg and end
as indicated, work Chart B over 100 sts, pm, work Chart C over 25 sts.
Work even in established pats until afghan measures approximately 64
inches, ending with Row 30 of Chart B.
Bind off.

Fringe

Cut strands of yarn each 12 inches long.

Holding 4 strands tog, fold each group in half.

Knot group into every 5th st along cast-on edge.

Rep along bound-off edge.

Trim fringe evenly. ◆

STITCH KEY

☐ K on RS, p on WS

⊟ P on RS, k on WS

Sl next 2 sts to cn and hold in front, p 2, k 2 from cn

Sl next 2 sts to cn and hold in back, k 2, p 2 from cn

Sl next 2 sts to cn and hold in front, k 2, k 2 from cn

Sl next 2 sts to cn and hold in back, k 2, k 2 from cn

Sl 2 sts to cn #1 and hold in back, sl 2 sts to cn #2 and hold in back, k 2 sts; k 2 sts from cn #2, p 2 sts from cn #1

Sl 2 sts to cn #1 and hold in front, sl next 2 sts to cn #2 and hold in front; p 2, k 2 sts from cn #2, k 2 sts from cn #1

Note: Only RS rows are shown on chart; for WS rows, K the K sts and P the P sts.

CHART A

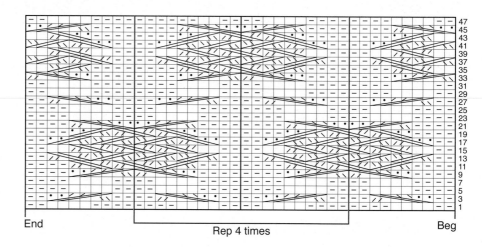

End

Rep 4 times

Beg

Note: Only RS rows are shown on chart; for WS rows, K the K sts and P the P sts.

CHART B

Note: Only RS rows are shown on chart; for WS rows, K the K sts and P the P sts.

CHART C

Cable **Blocks**

Design by E.J. Slayton

Four squares are knit together to create larger blocks in this carry-along project. Joining and borders can be worked at a leisurely pace.

Skill Level
Intermediate***

Size
Approximately 48 x 61 (64 x 79) inches
Instructions are given for smaller size, with larger sizes in parentheses. Each block of 4 squares measures approximately 15 inches.

Materials
- Brown Sheep Burly Spun, 100 percent wool super-bulky weight yarn (132 yds/8 oz per skein): 6 (9) skeins prairie fire #BS181 (A), 3 (8) skeins grey heather #BS03 (B), 3 (8) skeins cream #BS10 (C)
- Brown Sheep Nature Spun 100 percent wool worsted weight yarn (245 yds/100g per skein): 1 skein ash #720 (for seaming)
- Size 13 (9mm) straight and 32-inch circular needles or size needed to obtain gauge
- Cable needle
- Tapestry needle

Gauge
9 sts = 4 inches/10cm in garter st
Each cable square should measure approximately 8 inches square.
To save time, take time to check gauge.

Special Abbreviations
C2l (cable 2 left): Sl next 3 sts to cn and hold in front, k2, sl 3rd st on cn back to LH needle, p1, k2 from cn.
C2r (cable 2 right): Sl next 3 sts to cn and hold in back, k2, sl 3rd st on cn back to LH needle, p1, k2 from cn.
M1 (Make 1): Inc by making a backward loop over RH needle.

Pattern Stitch
Cable Square
Row 1 (WS): P1, k16, p1.
Row 2: K2, p2, k2, [p1, k1, M1] 4 times, p2, k2. (22 sts)
Rows 3, 5, 7 and 9: P2, k2, [p2, k1] 4 times, p2, k2, p2.
Row 4: K2, p2, k2, [p1, c2l] twice, p2, k2.
Row 6: K2, p2, [k2, p1] 4 times, k2, p2, k2.
Row 8: K2, p2, [c2r, p1] twice, k2, p2, k2.
Row 10: Rep Row 6.
Rows 11–18: Rep Rows 3–10.
Rows 19–21: Rep Rows 3–5.
Row 22: K2, p2, k2, [p1, ssk, p1, k2tog] twice, p2, k2. (18 sts)
Purling first and last sts, bind off knitwise on WS. Cut yarn.

Pattern Notes
First square of each block is cast on and knitted, then sts for squares 2, 3 and 4 are picked up and k along edge of the previous one. First and last squares are seamed tog (see Fig. 1 for direction of work and placement of colors).

To reduce bulk, worsted weight yarn is used for seams. Border is picked up and knitted after blocks are assembled. For ease in handling, designer suggests seaming 4 (5) blocks into lengthwise strips, then working side borders. Next, sew strips tog and work end borders, picking up first and last st in same st or space as first and last st of side borders.

Afghan

Block
Make 12 (20)
Square 1: With A, cast on 18 sts and work Cable Square.

Square 2: Holding square 1 with RS facing and bound-off edge at top, rotate ¼ turn clockwise. With B and working 1 st in from edge, pick up and k 18 sts along side edge of square; work another square.

Square 3: Rotate ¼ turn counterclockwise. With A, pick up and k 18 sts along side edge of square 2 as above.

Square 4: Rotate ¼ turn counterclockwise. With C, pick up and k 18 sts along side edge of square 3 as above.

With tapestry needle, sew seam between squares 1 and 4.

Finishing

Referring to Fig. 1, sew 4 (5) blocks into 3 (4) strips.

Border

With RS facing using A and circular needle, pick up and k 16 sts along side or end of each square in strip.

Row 1 (WS): P1, k to last st, p1.
Row 2: With C, k1, M1, k to last st, M1, k1.
Row 3: With C, rep Row 1.
Rows 4 and 5: With B, rep Rows 2 and 3.
Rows 6 and 7: With A, rep Rows 2 and 3.
Row 8: With A, k across.

Purling first and last sts, bind off knitwise on WS.

Rep Rows 1–8 for remaining edges.

Sew corners, working ½ st in from edge to give appearance of 1 St st at each corner.

Block lightly. ◆

COLOR KEY
■ Prairie fire (A)
▨ Grey heather (B)
□ Cream (C)

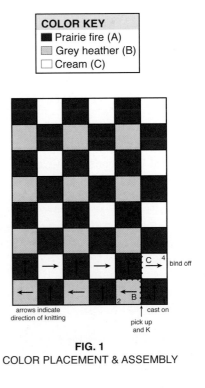

arrows indicate direction of knitting

pick up and K

cast on

FIG. 1
COLOR PLACEMENT & ASSEMBLY

Textured Diamonds

Design by E.J. Slayton

Diamond panels are set off by mirrored cables. This pattern gives the option of working from a chart or the written instructions.

Skill Level
Intermediate***

Size
Approximately 48 x 60 inches

Materials
- Brown Sheep Lamb's Pride Superwash Bulky, 100 percent washable wool bulky weight yarn (110 yds/100g per ball): 18 balls plum crazy #SW55
- Size 10½ (7mm) 29-inch circular needle or size needed to obtain gauge
- Stitch markers
- Cable needle
- Tapestry needle

Gauge
14 sts and 20 rows = 4 inches/10cm in Textured Diamonds pat
To save time, take time to check gauge.

Special Abbreviations
C4b (c4f): Sl next 4 sts to cn and hold in back (front), k4, k4 from cn.
M1 (Make 1): Inc by making a backward loop over RH needle.

Pattern Stitches
A. Textured Diamonds (multiple of 22 sts + 3)
Row 1 (RS): K2, *k1, p2, k2, p1, k3, p1, k1, p1, k3, p1, k2, p2, k2, rep from *, end k1.
Row 2: P1, *p2, k2, p2, k5, p1, k5, p2, k2, p1, rep from *, end p2.
Rows 3 and 5: K2, *p2, k2, [p1, k3] 3 times, p1, k2, p2, k1, rep from *, end k1.
Rows 4 and 6: P1, *p1, k2, p2, k5, p3, k5, p2, k2, rep from *, end p2.
Rows 7 and 9: K1, p1, *p1, k2, p1, k3, [p1, k2] twice, p1, k3, p1, k2, p2, rep from *, end k1.
Rows 8 and 10: P1, *k2, p2, k5, p2, k1, p2, k5, p2, k1, rep from *, end k1, p1.
Rows 11 and 13: K1, p1, *k2, p1, k3, p1, k2, p3, k2, p1, k3, p1, k2, p1, rep from *, end k1.
Rows 12 and 14: P1, *k1, p2, k5, p2, k3, p2, k5, p2, rep from *, end k1, p1.

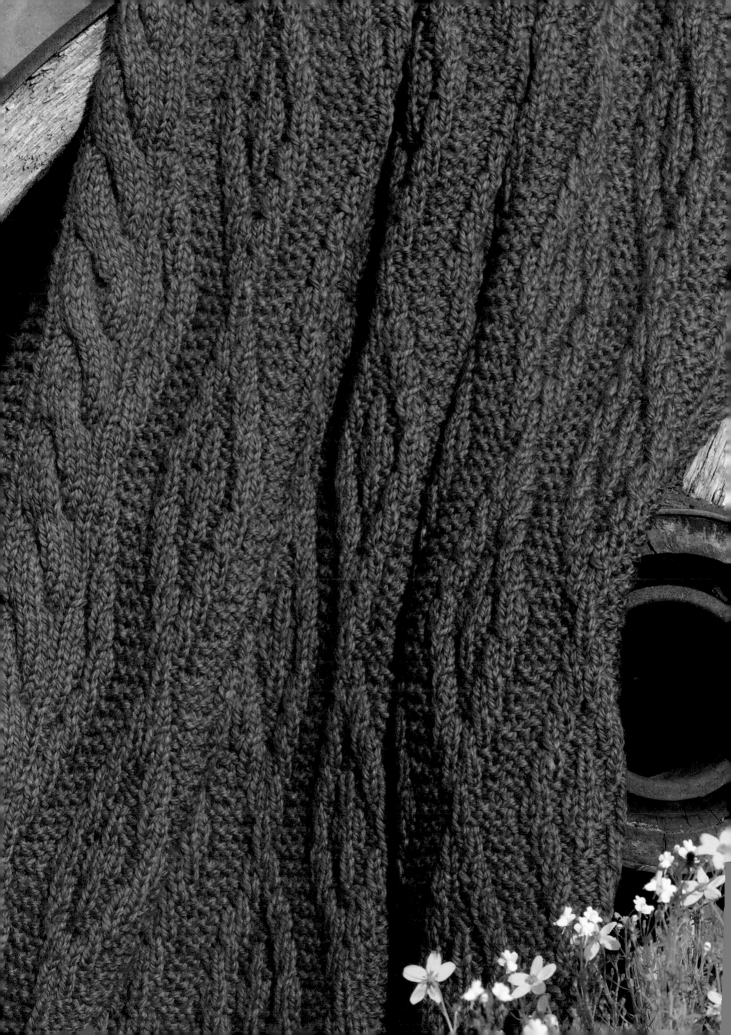

Rows 15 and 17: K2, *k1, p1, k3, p1, k2, p2, k1, p2, k2, p1, k3, p1, k2, rep from *, end k1.

Rows 16 and 18: P1, *p2, k5, p2, k2, p1, k2, p2, k5, p1, rep from *, end p2.

Rows 19 and 21: K2, *p1, k3, p1, k2, p2, k3, p2, k2, p1, k3, p1, k1, rep from *, end k1.

Rows 20 and 22: P1, *p1, k5, p2, k2, p3, k2, p2, k5, rep from *, end p2.

Rows 23–26: Rep Rows 15–18.

Rows 27–30: Rep Rows 11–14.

Rows 31–34: Rep Rows 7–10.

Rows 35–38: Rep Rows 3–6.

Rows 39 and 40: Rep Rows 1 and 2.

Rep Rows 1–40 for pat.

Back (Front) Cross Cable (panel of 10 sts)

Rows 1 and 3 (RS): P1, k8, p1.

Row 2 and all WS rows: K1, p8, k1.

Row 5: P1, c4b (c4f), p1.

Rows 6, 8 and 10: P1, k8, p1.

Rep Rows 1–10 for pat.

Pattern Notes

Circular needle is used to accommodate large number of sts. Do not join; work in rows.

Sl first st of garter-st edge purlwise at beg of RS rows for right panel and beg of WS rows for left panel.

Work Pat B (Back Cross Cable) on right panel; Pat C (Front Cross Cable) on left panel.

Afghan

Right Panel

Cast on 78 sts.

Border

Rows 1, 3 and 5 (WS): P1, k to end of row.

Rows 2, 4 and 6: Sl 1, k to end of row.

Row 7: P1, pm, k1, [M1, k1] 4 times, k1, pm, k next 60 sts inc 9 sts evenly, pm, k1, [M1, k1] 4 times, k1, pm, p1, k4. (95 sts)

Beg pat: Sl 1, k4, pm, work Row 1 of Pat B across 10 sts, Row 1 of Pat A across 69 sts, Row 1 of Pat B across 10 sts, k1.

Maintaining established cables, work Rows 1–40 of Pat A until afghan measures approximately 59

inches, ending with Row 20.

Dec row: Sl 1, k4, p1, dec 4 sts across top of cable, p1, k to next marker, dec 9 sts evenly, p1, dec 4 sts across top of cable, p1, k1. (78 sts)

Rep Rows 1–5 of border. Bind off purlwise on RS.

Left Panel

Cast on and work as for right panel, except place garter edge at beg of WS rows, and work Pat C (Front Cross Cable) instead of Pat B throughout.

Finishing

Lay panels with St st edges tog. Working 1 st in from edge, join panels.

Block lightly. ◆

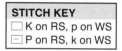

STITCH KEY
☐ K on RS, p on WS
⊟ P on RS, k on WS

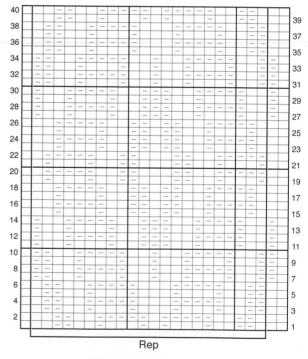

Rep

TEXTURED DIAMONDS CHART

Basketweave & Cable

Design by E.J. Slayton

This throw features a deeply textured knit-and-purl pattern, accented with matching cables. The pattern forms its own non-rolling end borders.

Skill Level
Intermediate***

Size
Approximately 38 x 60 (44½ x 75) inches
Instructions are given for smaller size, with larger size in parentheses. When only 1 number is given, it applies to both sizes.

Materials
- Brown Sheep Prairie Silks, 72 percent wool/18 percent mohair/10 percent silk worsted weight yarn (88 yds/50g per skein): 30 (42) skeins green back #PS850
- Size 10½ (6.5mm) 32-inch circular needle
- Size 11 (8mm) 29-inch circular needle or size needed to obtain gauge
- Stitch markers
- Cable needle
- Tapestry needle

Gauge
10 sts and 14 rows = 4 inches/10cm in Double Basketweave pat with larger needles and 2 strands of yarn held tog
To save time, take time to check gauge.

Special Abbreviations
C3b (cable 3 back): Sl next 3 sts to cn and hold in back, k3, k3 from cn.
C3b (cable 3 front): Sl next 3 sts to cn and hold in front, k3, k3 from cn.
C3l (cable 3 left): Sl next st to cn and hold in back, k3, p1 from cn.
C3r (cable 3 right): Sl next 3 sts to cn and hold in front, p1, k3 from cn.
M1 (Make 1): Inc by making a backward loop over RH needle.

Pattern Stitches
A. Double Basketweave (multiple of 18 sts + 10)
Row 1 (RS): K11, *p2, k2, p2, k12, rep from * across, end last rep k11.
Row 2: P1, *k8, [p2, k2] twice, p2, rep from *, end k8, p1.
Row 3: K1, *p8, [k2, p2] twice, k2, rep from *, end p8, k1.
Row 4: P11, *k2, p2, k2, p12, rep from * across, end last rep p11.
Rows 5–8: Rep Rows 1–4.
Row 9: Knit.
Row 10: [P2, k2] twice, *p12, [k2, p2] twice.
Row 11: K2, [p2, k2] twice, *p8, k2, [p2, k2] twice, rep from * across.
Row 12: P2, [k2, p2] twice, *k8, p2, [k2, p2] twice, rep from * across.
Row 13: [K2, p2] twice, *k12, [p2, k2] twice, rep from * across.
Rows 14–16: Rep Rows 10–12.
Row 17: Rep Row 13.
Row 18: Purl.
Rep Rows 1–18 for pat.

B. Garter St Cable (panel of 16 sts)

Rows 1 and 3 (RS): P2, k12, p2.

Rows 2, 4 and 6: K2, p12, k2.

Row 5: P2, c3b, c3f, p2.

Rows 7–10: Rep Rows 3–6.

Row 11: P1, c3r, p6, c3l, p1.

Row 12: K1, p3, k8, p3, k1.

Row 13: P1, k14, p1.

Row 14: K1, p14, k1.

Row 15: P1, k3, p8, k3, p1.

Row 16: Rep Row 12.

Row 17: P1, c3l, k6, c3r, p1.

Row 18: K2, p12, k2.

Row 19: Rep Row 5.

Rep Rows 2–19 for pat.

Pattern Notes

Circular needle is used to accommodate large number of sts. Do not join; work in rows.

Afghan is worked with 2 strands of yarn held tog throughout.

Sl first st of every row purlwise wyif.

Afghan

With smaller needle and double strand of yarn, cast on 116 (134) sts.

Border

Row 1 (WS): Sl 1, k3, p1, k1, pm, p2, [k2, p2] twice, k8, p2, [k2, p2] twice, pm, k2, [p2, k2] twice, pm, p2, [k2, p2] twice, [k8, p2, {k2, p2} twice] 1 (2) times, pm, k2, [p2, k2] twice, pm, p2, [k2, p2] twice, k8, p2, [k2, p2] twice, pm, k1, p1, k4.

Row 2: Sl 1, k4, k the knit sts, p the purl sts to last 6 sts, end p1, k5.

Row 3: Rep Row 1.

Row 4: Sl 1, k4, p1, [k2, p2] twice, k12, [p2, k2] 7 times, [k10, {p2, k2} twice] 1 (2) times, [p2, k2] 4 times, p2, k12, [p2, k2] twice, p1, k5.

Row 5: Sl 1, k3, p1, k1, p28, k2, [M1, p1] 6 times, k2, p28 (46), k2, [M1, p1] 6 times, k2, p28, k1, p1, k4. (128, 146 sts)

Beg pat (RS): Sl 1, k4, p1, work Row 1 of Double Basketweave pat across 28 sts, Row 1 of Garter St Cable pat across 16 sts, Row 1 of Double Basketweave pat across 28 (46) sts, Row 1 of Garter St Cable pat across 16 sts, Row 1 of Double Basketweave pat across 28 sts, end k1, p1, k4.

Change to larger needle and work in established pats until afghan measures approximately 59 (74) inches, ending with Row 8 of pats.

Top Border

Change to smaller needle.

Dec row (RS): Sl 1, k4, p1, work Row 9 of Double Basketweave pat across 28 sts, p2, [ssk] twice, [p2tog] twice, [k2tog] twice, p2, work Row 9 of Double Basketweave pat across 28 (46) sts, p2, [ssk] twice, [p2tog] twice, [k2tog] twice, p2, work Row 9 of Double Basketweave pat across 28 sts, end p1, k5.

Work Rows 10–12 of Double Basketweave pat in established panels, keeping cable sts in ribbing.

Bind off all sts in pat.

Block lightly. ◆

Cables & Diamonds

Design by Susan Robicheau

Cables combine with diamonds in diverse forms to create an attractive textured throw.

Skill Level
Advanced****

Size
Approximately 48 x 58 inches

Materials
- Brown Sheep Lamb's Pride Superwash Worsted, 100 percent washable wool worsted weight yarn (200 yds/100g per skein): 14 skeins Oats 'n Cream #SW115
- Size 13 (9mm) 36-inch circular needle or size needed to obtain gauge
- Cable needle
- Slze H/8 crochet hook
- Stitch markers

Gauge
11 sts and 13 rows = 4 inches/10cm in St st with 2 strands of yarn
To save time, take time to check gauge.

Special Abbreviations
C2f (cable 2 front): Sl next st to cn and hold in front, k1, k1 from cn.
C2b (cable 2 back): Sl next st to cn and hold in back, k1, k1 from cn.
Pc2f (purl cable 2 front): Sl next st to cn and hold in front, p1, k1 from cn.
Pc2b (purl cable 2 back): Sl next st to cn and hold in back, k1, p1 from cn.
Sl-1f: Sl next st to cn and hold in front.
Sl-1b: Sl next st to cn and hold in front.
Sl-2f: Sl next 2 sts to cn and hold in front.

Sl-2b: Sl next 2 sts to cn and hold in front.

Pattern Stitches
Border
Row 1 (RS): *P9, k1, p8, rep from * across row.
Row 2 and all WS rows: K and p the sts as they present themselves.
Row 3: *P8, k3, p7, rep from * across row.
Row 5: *P7, k3, p1, k1, p6, rep from * across row.
Row 7: *P6, k5, p1, k1, p5, rep from * across row.
Row 9: *P5, k5, [p1, k1] twice, p4, rep from * across row.
Row 11: *P4, k7, [p1, k1] twice, p3, rep from * across row.
Row 13: *P3, k7, [p1, k1] 3 times, p2, rep from * across row.
Row 15: *P2, k9, p1, [k1, p1] 3 times, rep from * across row.
Row 17: *P1, k9, [p1, k1] 4 times, rep from * across row.
Row 19: *K9, p1, [k1, p1] 4 times, rep from * across row.
Row 21: *K8, p3, k1, [p1, k1] 3 times, rep from * across row.
Row 23: *K7, p5, [k1, p1] 3 times, rep from * across row.
Row 25: *K6, p7, k1, [p1, k1] twice, rep from * across row.
Row 27: *K5, p9, [k1, p1] twice, rep from * across row.
Row 29: *K4, p11, k1, p1, k1, rep from *

across row.

Row 31: *K3, p13, k1, p1, rep from * across row.

Row 33: *K2, p15, k1, rep from * across row.

Row 35: *K1, p17, rep from * across row.

Row 36: *K17, p1, rep from * across row.

A. Diamonds & Triangles (Panel of 23 sts)

Row 1 (RS): K4, p5, c2b, k1, c2f, p5, k4.

Row 2: [P5, k4] twice, p5.

Row 3: K6, p2, c2b, k3, c2f, p2, k6.

Row 4: [P7, k1] twice, p7.

Row 5: K2, p5, c2b, k5, c2f, p5, k2.

Row 6: P3, k4, p9, k4, p3.

Row 7: K4, p2, c2b, p7, c2f, p2, k4.

Row 8: P5, k1, p2, k7, p2, k1, p5.

Row 9: K5, c2b, k2, p5, k2, c2f, p5.

Row 10: P1, k4, p4, k5, p4, k4, p1.

Row 11: K2, p2, c2b, k4, p3, k4, c2f, p2, k2.

Row 12: P3, k1, p6, k3, p6, k1, p3.

Row 13: K3, c2b, k6, p1, k6, c2f, k3.

Row 14: P11, k1, p11.

Row 15: K4, p7, k1, p7, k4.

Row 16: P4, k7, p1, k7, p4.

Row 17: K3, c2f, p5, k3, p5, c2b, k3.

Row 18: P3, k1, p1, k5, p3, k5, p1, k1, p3.

Row 19: K2, p2, pc2f, p3, k5, p3, pc2b, p2, k2.

Row 20: P1, k4, p1, k3, p5, k3, p1, k4, p1.

Row 21: P5, pc2f, p1, k7, p1, pc2b, p5.

Row 22: P5, k1, p1, k1, p7, k1, p1, k1, p5.

Row 23: K4, p2, pc2f, p7, pc2b, p2, k4.

Row 24: P3, k4, p1, k7, p1, k4, p3.

Row 25: K2, p5, pc2f, p5, pc2b, p5, k2.

Row 26: P7, k1, p1, k5, p1, k1, p7.

Row 27: K6, p2, pc2f, p3, pc2b, p2, k6.

Row 28: P5, k4, p1, k3, p1, k4, p5.

Row 29: K4, p5, pc2f, p1, pc2b, p5, k4.

Row 30: P11, k1, p11.

Row 31: K10, sl-2b, k1, k2 from cn, k10.

Row 32: Purl.

Rep Rows 1–32 for pat.

B. Seeded Cable (Panel of 12 sts)

Row 1 (RS): K3, p1, [k1, p1] twice, k4.

Row 2: P3, k1, [p1, k1] twice, p4.

Rows 3–8: Rep Rows 1–2.

Row 9: Sl 3 sts to cn and hold in back, p1, k1, p1, then k3 from cn; sl 3 to cn and hold in front, k3, then k1, p1, k1 from cn.

Row 10: K1, p1, k1, p7, k1, p1.

Row 11: P1, k1, p1, k7, p1, k1.

Rows 12–18: Rep Rows 10 and 11.

Row 19: Sl 3 sts to cn and hold at back of work, k3, then p1, k1, p1 from cn; sl 3 to cn and hold in front, k1, p1, k1, then k3 from cn.

Row 20: P3, k1, [p1, k1] twice, p4.

Rep Rows 1–20 for pat.

C. Entwined Diamonds

Row 1 (RS): P2, sl-1b, k1, p1 from cn, sl-1f, p1, k1 from cn, p7, sl-1b, k2, k1 from cn, sl-2f, k1, k2 from cn, p7, sl-1b, k1, p1 from cn, sl-1f, p1, k1 from cn, p2.

Row 2 and all WS rows: K or p the sts as they present themselves.

Row 3: P1, sl-1b, k1, p1 from cn, p2, sl-1f, p1, k1 from cn, p5, sl-1b, k2, k1 from cn, k2, sl-2f, k1, k1 from cn, p5, sl-1b, k1, p1 cn, p2, sl-1f, p1, k1 from cn, p1.

Row 5: Sl-1b, p1, k1 from cn, p4, sl-1f, p1, k1 from cn, p3, sl-1b, k2, p1 from cn, sl-2b, k2, k2 from cn, sl-2f, p1, k2 from cn, p3, sl-1b, k1, p1 from cn, p4, sl-1f, p1, k1 from cn.

Row 7: Sl-1f, p1, k1 from cn, p4, sl-1b, k1, p1 from cn, p2, sl-1b, k2, p1 from cn, sl-2f, p1, k2 from cn, p2, sl-1f, p1, k1 from cn, p4, sl-1b, k1, p1 from cn.

Row 9: P1, sl-1f, p1, k1 from cn, p2, sl-1b, k1, p1 from cn, p2, sl-1b, k2, p1 from cn, sl-1b, k2, p1 from cn, p2, sl-2f, p1, k2 from cn, sl-2f, p1, k2 from cn, p2, sl-1f, p1, k1 from cn, p2, sl-1b, k1, p1 from cn.

Row 11: P2, sl-1f, p1, k1 from cn, p2, sl-1b, k2, p1 from cn, sl-1b, k2, p1 from cn, p4, sl-2f, p1, k2 from cn, sl-2f, p1, k2 from cn, p2, sl-1f, p1, k1 from cn, sl-1b, k1, p1 from cn, p2.

Row 13: P3, sl-1b, k1, k1 from cn, p2, sl-1b, k2, p1 from cn, sl-1b, k2, k1 from cn, p6, sl-2f, k1, k2 from cn, sl-2f, p1, k2 from cn, p2, sl-1b, k1, k1 from cn, p3.

Row 15: P6, sl-1b, k2, p1 from cn, sl-1b, k2, k1 from cn, sl-1f, k1, k1 from cn, p4, sl-1b, k1, k1 from cn, sl-2f, k1, k2 from cn, sl-2f, p1, k2 from cn, p6.

Row 17: P5, sl-1b, k2, p1 from cn, sl-1b, k2, k1 from cn, k2, sl-1f, k1, k1 from cn, p2, sl-1b, k1, k1 from cn, k2, sl-2f, k1, k2 from cn, sl-2f, p1, k2 from cn, p5.

Row 19: P4, sl-1b, k2, p1 from cn, sl-1b, k2, k1 from cn, k4, sl-1f, k1, k1 from cn, sl-1b, k1, k1 from cn, k4, sl-2f, k1, k2 from cn, sl-2f, p1, k2 from cn, p4.

Row 21: P3, sl-1b, k2, p1 from cn, p1, sl-2f, p1, k2 from cn, k5, sl-1b, k1, k1 from cn, k5, sl-1b, k2, p1 from cn, p1, sl-2f, p1, k2 from cn, p3.

Row 23: P2, sl-1b, k1, p1 from cn, sl-1f, p1, k1 from cn, p2, sl-2f, p1, k2 from cn, k10, sl-1b, k2, p1 from cn, p2, sl-1b, k1, p1 from cn, sl-1f, p1, k1 from cn, p2.

Row 25: P1, sl-1b, k1, p1 from cn, p2, sl-1f, p1, k1 from cn, p2, sl-2f, p1, k2 from cn, k8, sl-1b, k2, p1 from cn, p2, sl-1b, k1, p1 from cn, p2, sl-1f, p1, k1 from cn, p1.

Row 27: Sl-1b, k1, p1 from cn, p4, sl-1f, p1, k1 from cn, p2, sl-2f, p1, k2 from cn, k6, sl-1b, k2, p1 from cn, p2, sl-1b, k1, p1 from cn, p4, sl-1f, p1, k1 from cn.

Row 29: Sl-1f, p1, k1 from cn, p2, sl-1b, k1, p1 from cn, p3, sl-2f, p1, k2 from cn, k4, sl-1b, k2, p1 from cn, p3, sl-1f, p1, k1 from cn, p4, sl-1b, k1, p1 from cn.

Row 31: P1, sl-1f, p1, k1 from cn, p2, sl-1b, k1, p1 from cn, p5, sl-2f, p1, k2 from cn, k2, sl-1b, k2, p1 from cn, p5, sl-1f, p1, k1 from cn, p2, sl-1b, k1, p1 from cn, p1.

Row 33: P2, sl-1f, p1, k1 from cn, sl-1b, k1, p1 from cn, p7, sl-2f, p1, k2 from cn, sl-1b, k2, p1 from cn, p7, sl-1f, p1, k1 from cn, sl-1b, k1, p1 from cn, p2.

Row 35: P3, sl-1b, k1, k1 from cn, p9, sl-2b, k2, k2 from cn, p9, sl-1b, k1, k1 from cn, p3.

Row 36: Rep Row 2.

Pattern Notes

Two strands of yarn are held tog for entire afghan. Circular needle is used to accommodate large number of sts. Do not join; work in rows.

Afghan

Cast on 126 sts
Rows 1 and 3 (RS): Purl.
Rows 2 and 4: Knit.
Work Rows 1–36 of Border pat.
Next row (RS): Purl, inc 18 sts evenly. (144 sts)
Knit 1 row.

Center Section

Set up pat (RS): K7, work Row 1 of pat A over 23 sts, pm, k7, pm, work Row 1 of pat B over 12 sts, pm, k7, pm, work Row 1 of pat C over 32 sts, pm, k7, pm, work Row 1 of pat B over 12 sts, pm, k7, pm, work Row 1 of pat A over 23 sts, pm, k7.
Continue to work even in established pats until 3 reps of pat C have been complete. (108 rows)
Next row (RS): Purl, dec 18 sts evenly. (126 sts)
Knit 1 row.
Work Rows 1–36 of Border pat.
Work in reverse St st for 4 rows.
Bind off, do not cut yarn.

Finishing

Place last st on crochet hook and work 1 rnd of sc around entire afghan, working 3 sc in each corner st and making sure to keep work flat.
Join with sl st. Fasten off. ◆

Twilight Skies

Design by E.J. Slayton

The rich shades of twilight accentuate a deeply cabled throw. Make the larger size if you prefer a full-size afghan.

Skill Level
Intermediate***

Size
Approximately 32 x 60 (44 x 73) inches
Instructions are given for smaller size, with larger size in parentheses. When only 1 number is given, it applies to both sizes.

Materials
- Brown Sheep Handpaint Originals, 70 percent mohair/30 percent wool worsted weight yarn (88 yds/50g per skein): 18 (30) skeins peacock #HP65 (A), 9 (15) skeins stormy skies #HP90 (B)
- Size 15 (10mm) 32-inch circular needle or size needed to obtain gauge
- Cable needle
- Stitch markers
- Tapestry needle

Gauge
8 sts and 11 rows = 4 inches/10cm in St st with 3 strands of yarn held tog
To save time, take time to check gauge.

Special Abbreviations
M1 (Make 1): Inc by making a backward loop over RH needle.
Bc (back cross): Sl next 3 sts to cn and hold in back, k3, k3 from cn.
Fc (front cross): Sl next 3 sts to cn and hold in front, k3, k3 from cn.

Pattern Stitch
Cables (multiple of 14 sts + 8)
Row 1 and all WS rows: K1, *p6, k1, rep from * across row.

Row 2: P1, fc, p1, *k6, p1, fc, p1, rep from * across row.
Row 4: P1, *k6, p1, rep from * across row.
Row 6: P1, k6, p1, *bc, p1, k6, p1, rep from * across row.
Rows 8 and 10: Rep Row 4.
Row 12: Rep Row 6.
Row 14: Rep Row 4.
Row 16: Rep Row 2.
Rows 18 and 20: Rep Row 4.
Rep Rows 1–20 for pat.

Pattern Notes
Afghan is worked with 2 strands of A and 1 strand of B held tog throughout.
Circular needles are used to accommodate large number of sts. Do not join; work in rows.
Sl first st of every row purlwise wyif.

Afghan
Cast on 58 (76) sts.
Rows 1–5: Sl 1, knit to end of row.
Set up row (RS): Sl 1, k3, pm, p1, [k1, M1] 3 times, p1, *k1, M1, k2, M1, k1, p1, [k1, M1] 3 times, p1, rep from * to last 4 sts, pm, end k4. (86, 114 sts)
Beg pat: Sl 1, k3, work Row 1 of pat to last 4 sts, end k4.
Maintaining borders, work in established pat until afghan measures approximately 59 (72) inches, ending with Row 3.
Dec row: Sl 1, k3, p1, ssk, [k2tog] twice, p1, *k1, ssk, k2tog, k1, p1, ssk, [k2tog] twice, p1, rep from * to last 4 sts, end k4. (58, 76 sts)
Continuing to sl first st of every row, knit 4 rows.
Bind off knitwise on WS. ◆

Flying Cables

Design by Barbara Venishnick

Increases and decreases in the areas between cables form a natural scallop along the edges of this afghan.

Skill Level
Easy**

Size
Approximately 44 x 59 inches

Materials
- Brown Sheep Lamb's Pride Worsted, 85 percent wool/15 percent mohair worsted weight yarn (190 yds/4 oz per hank): 6 hanks blue heirloom #M75
- Brown Sheep Handpaint Originals 70 percent mohair/30 percent wool worsted weight yarn (88 yds/50g per hank): 12 hanks tropical water #HP60
- Size 15 (10mm) 29-inch circular needle or size needed to obtain gauge
- Cable needle

Gauge
9 sts and 13 rows = 4 inches/10cm in St st with 2 strands of yarn held tog
To save time, take time to check gauge.

Special Abbreviation
C6f (cable 6 front): Sl 3 sts to cn and hold in front, k3, k3 from cn.

Pattern Stitch
Flying Cables
Rows 1, 3, 7, 9 and 13 (RS): K1-tbl, [k1, p1, k6, p1, k1, ssk, k4, yo, k1, yo, k4, k2tog] 5 times, k1, p1, k6, p1, k1, sl 1 wyif.
Rows 2, 4, 6, 8, 10 and 12: K1-tbl, [p1, k1, p6, k1, p14] 5 times, p1, k1, p6, k1, p1, sl 1 wyif.
Row 5: K1-tbl, [k1, p1, c6f, p1, k1, ssk, k4, yo, k1, yo, k4, k2tog] 5 times, k1, p1, c6f, p1, k1, sl 1 wyif.
Row 11: Rep Row 5.
Row 14: K1-tbl, [p1, k1, p6, k1, {p1, k6} twice] 5 times, p1, k1, p6, k1, p1, sl 1 wyif.
Rep Rows 1–14 for pat.

Pattern Notes
One strand of each color are held tog for entire afghan.
Circular needle is used to accommodate large number of sts. Do not join; work in rows.

Afghan
With 2 strands of yarn held tog, cast on 127 sts.
[Work Rows 1–14 of Flying Cables pat] 14 times, rep Rows 1–13.
Bind off knitwise on WS.
Block. ◆

Wishbone

Design by Barbara Venishnick

Chunky cables on a seed stitch background
highlight a brawny afghan.

Skill Level
Easy**

Size
Approximately 46 x 58, excluding fringe

Materials
- Brown Sheep Burly Spun, 100 percent wool super-bulky weight yarn (132 yds/8 oz per hank): 8 hanks fuchsia #BS23
- Size 17 (12mm) 29-inch circular needle or size needed to obtain gauge
- Cable needle
- Size G/6 crochet hook for placing fringe

Gauge
8 sts and 12 rows = 4 inches/10cm in Seed Stitch Rib pat
To save time, take time to check gauge.

Special Abbreviations
C4b (cable 4 back): Sl 2 sts to cn and hold in back, k2, k2 from cn.
C4f (cable 4 front): Sl 2 sts to cn and hold in front, k2, k2 from cn.

Pattern Stitch
Seed Stitch Rib
Rows 1, 5 and 7 (RS): [K1, p1] 3 times, [k8, {p1, k1} 8 times, p1] 3 times, k8, [p1, k1] 3 times.

Row 2 and all WS rows: P5, [k1, p8, k1, p15] 3 times, k1, p8, k1, p5.
Row 3: [K1, p1] 3 times, [c4b, c4f, {p1, k1} 8 times, p1] 3 times, c4b, c4f, [p1, k1] 3 times.
Row 8: Rep Row 2.
Rep Rows 1–8 for pat.

Pattern Note
Circular needle is used to accommodate large number of sts. Do not join; work in rows.

Afghan
Cast on 95 stitches.
Work even in Seed Stitch Rib pat until afghan measures approximately 58 inches, ending with Row 4 of pat.
Bind off.

Fringe
Cut 190 strands of yarn, each 12 inches long.
Fold 1 strand in half and knot in each Row 1 st at beg of afghan just above cast-on edge.
Pull tails through folded loop and pull tightly.
Rep fringe in each Row 4 st just below bound-off edge. ◆

Meandering Cables

Design by Kennita Tully

The cables that wander back and forth on this afghan imitate the meanderings of a stream. The aquamarine color repeats this theme.

Skill Level
Intermediate***

Size
Approximately 38 x 46 inches

Materials
- Brown Sheep Lamb's Pride Superwash Bulky, 100 percent washable wool bulky weight wool yarn (110 yds/100g per skein): 9 skeins each aquamarine # SW155 and stonewashed denim #SW150.
- Size 15 (10mm) needles or size needed to obtain gauge
- Cable needle
- Tapestry needle

Gauge
12 sts and 12 rows = 4 inches/10cm in cable pattern
To save time, take time to check gauge.

Special Abbreviations
Fc (front cross): Sl 2 sts to cn and hold in front, k2, k2 from cn.
Bc (back cross): Sl 2 sts to cn and hold in back, k2, k2 from cn.
Inc: Purl into front and back of same stitch.

Pattern Stitch
Meandering Cable (panel of 16 sts)
Rows 1, 3 and 5 (WS): P2, k2, p4, k6, p2.
Row 2: K2, p6, k4, p2, k2.
Row 4: K2, p6, fc, p2, k2.
Row 6: K2, p4, p2tog, k4, inc, p1, k2.

Row 7 and all following WS rows: K the knit and inc sts, p the purl sts.
Row 8: K2, p5, fc, p3, k2.
Row 10: K2, p3, p2tog, k4, inc, p2, k2.
Row 12: K2, p4, fc, p4, k2.
Row 14: K2, p2, p2tog, k4, inc, p3, k2.
Row 16: K2, p3, fc, p5, k2.
Row 18: K2, p1, p2tog, k4, inc, p4, k2.
Row 20: K2, p2, fc, p6, k2.
Row 22: K2, p2, k4, p6, k2.
Row 24: K2, p2, bc, p6, k2.
Row 26: K2, p1, inc, k4, p2tog, p4, k2.
Row 28: K2, p3, bc, p5, k2.
Row 30: K2, p2, inc, k4, p2tog, p3, k2.
Row 32: K2, p4, bc, p4, k2.
Row 34: K2, p3, inc, k4, p2tog, p2, k2.
Row 36: K2, p5, bc, p3, k2.
Row 38: K2, p4, inc, k4, p2tog, p1, k2.
Row 40: K2, p6, bc, p2, k2.
Rep Rows 1–40 for pat.

Pattern Note
Hold 1 strand of each color tog for entire afghan.

Afghan
Cast on 4 sts. Knit 2 rows.

Row 1 (RS): K2, insert RH ndl from front to back into the yarn running between RH ndl and LH ndl, [yo] twice and pull through, k2.

Panel A
Make 4
Cast on 16 sts.
Beg with Row 1, work 3½ reps of cable pat, ending with Row 20.
Bind off in pat.

Panel B
Make 4
Cast on 16 sts.
Beg with Row 21, work 3½ reps of cable pat, ending with Row 40.
Bind off in pat.

Finishing
Block each panel.
Referring to Fig. 1, sew panels together with Mattress stitch.
Block lightly again. ◆

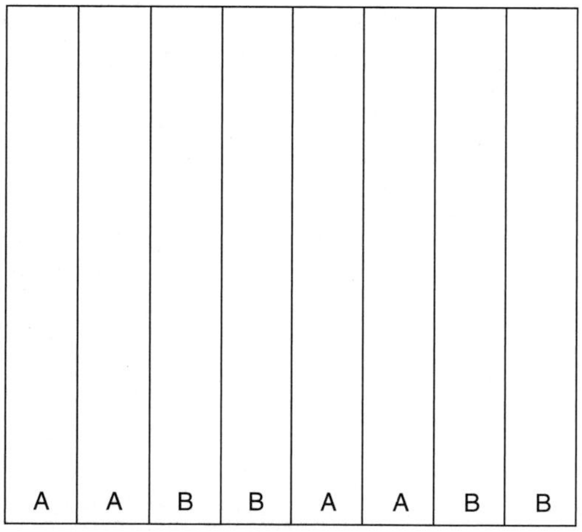

FIG. 1
ASSEMBLY

Lace Lily Throw

Design by Diane Zangl

Five shaped panels are joined with crochet loops to create an airy throw that is also cozy and warm.

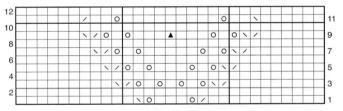

Skill Level
Intermediate***

Size
Approximately 50 x 57 inches

Materials
- Brown Sheep Nature Spun, 100 percent wool worsted weight yarn (245 yd/100g per skein): 9 skeins pink please #N98 (MC), 4 skeins cranberry fog #N81 (CC)
- Size 10½ (6.5mm) needles or size needed to obtain gauge
- Size G/6 crochet hook
- Stitch markers

Gauge
14 sts and 16 rows = 4 inches/10cm in St st

29-st panel = 8 inches, blocked without edging

Special Abbreviations
M1L (Make 1 Left): Make a clockwise backwards loop and place on RH needle.
M1R (Make 1 Right): Make a counterclockwise loop and place on RH needle. On next row, k in the back of this st to avoid a hole.

Panel
Make 5
With 2 strands of MC held tog, cast on 19 sts.
Row 1 (WS): Purl.
Row 2: K1, M1L, k to last st, M1R, k1.
[Rep Rows 1-2] 4 times more. (29 sts)
Purl 1 row. Mark last inc on each end.
[Work 12 rows of chart] 16 times. Panel measures approximately 52 inches.

LACE LILY CHART

STITCH KEY
- ☐ K on RS, p on WS
- ⊙ Yo
- ▲ Bobble: [K, p, k] in same st, turn, p3, turn, sl 1, k2tog, psso
- ◥ Ssk
- ◿ K2tog

Shape end
Row 1 (RS): K1, ssk, k to last 3 sts, k2tog, k.
Row 2: Purl. Mark first dec on each end.
[Rep Rows 1-2] 4 times more. (19 sts)
Bind off.
Block.

Border
With 2 strands of CC held tog, work 1 sc in each row or st around entire panel.
Rnd 2: *Ch 5, sk 2 sc, sl st in next sc; rep from * around. Join with sl st.
Re-mark each ch-5 loop opposite shaping markers. There will be 13 loops between markers on each shaped end. Rep for remaining panels.

Join Panels
With each panel facing in opposite directions, join CC in one marked loop.
Ch 3, sl st in marked loop of 2nd panel, *ch 3, sl st in next loop of opposite panel; rep from * to end joining last marked loops.
Fasten off.
Rep with remaining panels.

Picot Edging
Join CC in any loop. *2 sc in ch-5 loop, ch 2, sl st in first ch, 2 sc in ch-5 loop. Rep from * to joining band, work 2 sc in each loop of joining band*. Rep from * to * around entire throw.
Join with sl st. Fasten off.
Block. ◆

Special **Thanks**

We would like to thank Brown Sheep Co. for providing all the yarn used in this book. We also appreciate the help provided by Peggy Jo Wells and the Brown Sheep staff throughout the publishing process. It's been great working with them. We also thank the talented knitting designers whose work is featured in this collection.

JC Briar
Nature's First Green, 115

Dixie Butler
Five Easy Cables, 136
Gray Rose, 76

Kathy Cheifetz
Chocolate Mousse, 138

Sue Childress
Strawberry Parfait, 12
Sweet Scallops, 10

Liliane Dickinson
April Showers, 24

Joyce Englund
Celtic Tradition, 144
Dimensional Triangles, 140
Ruble Red, 142

Nazanin S. Fard
Autumn Blaze, 118
Diamond Lace, 78
Star Quilt, 27

Jacqueline W. Hoyle
Bells & Lace, 30

Frances Hughes
Confetti, 14
Hyacinth Beauty, 124
Linked Chains, 146

Katharine Hunt
Climbing Vines, 126
Criss-Cross Diamonds, 67
Kid's Cabin Coverlet, 33
Openwork Lattice, 70
Sporty Squares, 62
Wings & Waves, 64

Kathleen Power Johnson
English Garden, 121
Flora Dora, 112

Melissa Leapman
Misty Blue, 148
Romantic Ruby, 134

Carolyn Pfeifer
Lavender Mist, 52

Janet Rehfeldt
Jewel Tones, 54
Little Gems, 18
Morning Sunlight, 16

Susan Robicheau
A Winter's Day, 86
Cables & Diamonds, 160
Summer Meadow, 50
Tulip Time, 108

Kathleen Sasser
Heart of Mine, 20

Mary Saunders
Field of Pansies, 22

Jean Schafer-Albers
Fence, 101
Flowers on the

E.J. Slayton
Basketweave &
Cable, 157
Cable Blocks, 151
Rio Grande Stripes, 44
Textured Diamonds, 154
Twilight Skies, 164

Kennita Tully
Baby Blocks, 42
Lollipops, 8
Meandering Cables, 170

Barbara Venishnick
Bamboo Fence, 56
Flying Cables, 166
Gingham Garden, 98
This Way & That Way, 36
Wishbone, 168

Lois S. Young
Bavarian Beauty, 80
Blossoms & Cables, 106
Blue Bells, 38
Bunches of Violets, 95
Diamond Lattice, 92
Dotted Stripes, 58
Wrapped in Ripples, 60

Diane Zangl
Lace Blocks, 40
Lace Lily Throw, 173
Navajo Trails, 73
Tile Paths, 83

Standard **Abbreviations**

beg .... begin(ning)
CC .... contrast color
ch .... chain
cn .... cable needle
dec .... decrease
dpn .... double-pointed needle
g .... gram(s)
inc .... increase
k .... knit
LH .... left hand
MC .... main color
oz .... ounce(s)
p .... purl
pat .... pattern
pm .... place marker
psso .... pass slipped stitch over knit (or purl) stitch
rep .... repeat
RH .... right hand
rnd .... round
RS .... right side

sl .... slip
ssk .... slip, slip, knit
(a left-slanting decrease): slip 2 stitches individually
as if to knit to right-hand needle, reinsert tip of left
needle and knit 2 stitches together through back loops

st(s) .... stitch(es)
St st .... Stockinette stitch
tbl .... through back loops
tog .... together
WS .... wrong side
wyib .... with yarn in back
wyif .... with yarn in front
yo .... yarn over
" .... inch(es)

* .... repeat instructions
from asterisk as directed

( ) .... repeat instructions
within brackets number of times stated